SCREENFARERS

SCREEN FARERS

Nurturing deliberate action in a digital world

Seth Bunev

cladonia
PRESS

Screenfarers: Nurturing Deliberate Action in a Digital World

© Seth Bunev, December 2020

Published in Canada by Cladonia Press. First print edition June 2021.

Paperback ISBN: 978-1-7774949-2-6

Other formats:

Ebook (US Letter PDF) ISBN: 978-1-7774949-0-2
Ebook (A4 PDF) ISBN: 978-1-7774949-1-9
Coilbound ISBN: 978-1-7774949-3-3

Cover, illustrations, and design by Seth Bunev. Diagrams created with <u>draw.io</u>.

screenfarers.com

Table of Contents

Directory of Exercises

Introduction

The technology of seafaring has many benefits, allowing societies to exchange goods and ideas across vast expanses of ocean. Yet there is a price. The sea is perhaps the most dangerous, lawless environment human beings inhabit.

Like the sea, the internet's fluidity makes it hard to pin down or regulate. Like the sea, the benefits it brings come interwoven with dangers.

This book is concerned with one aspect of those dangers: the ways that digital technologies reshape our minds. This shaping can happen unintentionally, but it is often deliberately orchestrated. A specific suite of psychological techniques, rampant throughout the digital realm, enables companies to create unwanted habits that can feel like addictions. As a result, digital platforms are devouring the lives of people all over the world, especially children and youth. That is what they are designed to do: capture time and attention in exchange for ad revenue.

We often refer to using the internet as 'surfing the web,' but the culture of the digital age has been one of surfing for long enough. To let the waves push us around where they will is to let tech companies shape our minds into whatever they find most profitable. It is time we put up sails, tack to the winds, and set out with intention and caution—ready to defend against attention pirates.

For a deep-sea excursion, a pair of board shorts is not sufficient equipment! Faced with the wild psychological frontier of the digital world, we need to develop a culture of deliberate navigation. We need an art of screenfaring.

I grew up on the leading edge of the internet wave. I remember a time when the internet was not the centre of everyone's existence. When I was in high school, a friend remarked: "Remember when we used to have hobbies?"

I did remember. Had I been born just a few years later, the answer might have been "what's a hobby?"

By that point, cellphones were ubiquitous among my teenage peers, smartphones were getting there, and we devoted most of our free time to our laptops. It was disconcerting to realise how much I depended on devices for simple tasks. I could hardly navigate my own neighbourhood without Google giving me directions, much less the transit system of my city. My memory was poor. I was always tired because I was often online until 3 AM. At one point, I realised I did not know how to make eye contact in a normal way. When I tried to figure it out, I realised none of my peers did either.

I was also disturbed by the link I experienced between excessive technology use and depression. I had friends who were affected even worse than I was, to the point of suicide attempts.

I was so disturbed that after I graduated high school, I stopped using Google. Instead of submitting my every thought to the search engine, I thought about the subject further. I was pleasantly surprised by what I came up with and how much I learned. And, when I finally did come across an answer to a question in a book or conversation, how much I remembered. At the end of the summer, I stowed my computer files on a USB drive—in case I needed them one day—and gave away my phone and laptop.

I thought I was getting rid of them forever. I lived abroad for a year, keeping in touch with friends and family entirely by handwritten letters. Then I went travelling. I navigated using an old compass, the position of the sun, maps, memories of maps, and directions from strangers (the strangers often googled the directions, after being puzzled that I didn't simply do this myself). I heard music only when it was performed in front of me, or when I played it myself. I learned songs from people that I met, not from YouTube.

The whole time, I was disentangling many of the ways the internet had affected my mind. Nothing makes such effects obvious like taking the devices away. There were so many skills I had never learned that a previous generation would have taken for granted: composing letters, finding information on the shelves of a library, social nuances, finding a building by address alone. Yet I was learning most of these skills with no role models.

Four years later, when I decided to go to university, I had to accept computer use back into my life. But this time, I was a little wiser. I strove to use this technology in a deliberate manner. I tested different ways of containing its effects, with varying degrees of success. I tried to use the internet without being used. I failed. I kept trying, and failing, and gradually began to succeed.

Meanwhile, I pored over research on the interactions between digital technology and the mind, from various disciplinary silos. I read industry research on how to make apps 'addictive,' psychological studies that tried to statistically determine if and how mental health is affected by tech (a field which appeared oddly ignorant of the existence of the industry research), anthropological research into how people experience digital devices, and neuroscience papers on how different interactions with digital technology rewire the brain.

These threads of research gradually wove into a more cohesive picture, in the light of my years of attention to the impacts of digital technology, conversations about these issues, and experiences teaching kids.

Much of the concern around excessive use of digital technology centres around the amount of time spent staring at screens and the like, with good reason. Screen time is easy to measure. In excess, it has relatively clear links to health impacts like eye strain and sleep disruption.

Unfortunately, 'screentime' does not give us much to work with when it comes to explaining the mental effects of digital technologies—or finding ways to mitigate harmful ones. We can reduce screentime, and sometimes this is a useful and appropriate approach. But a lot of the impact depends on how the screens are being used. What would it look like to do screentime *better*?

This is the question that *Screenfarers* attempts to answer. While drawing on different angles, this book comes at the issue with a focus on how we *experience* digital technologies, and how they shape our experience. As human beings, this is how each of us interacts with the world: we need tools that can be applied without neuroscience expertise or brain scanning equipment. That is what I have endeavored to create: a practical toolkit for separating the benefits of the internet age from the harms, and for teaching young people to do the same.

Screenfaring, like seafaring, requires discipline and work. It is not passive. You must keep a sharp lookout for reefs and rocks. You must understand the winds, tides, and currents to get where you want to go, and to avoid the dangers. You must plan a route in advance and keep the ship in good order.

It is worth the effort. Screenfaring enables adventure, trade, cooperation, and learning in ways that have never been possible before. A skillful screenfarer can reap these benefits, while *also* avoiding enslavement, hidden reefs, or a meeting with Davy Jones.

This book is for anyone who wishes to cultivate a more deliberate relationship with digital technologies. In particular, the book is addressed to teachers and parents in circumstances where laptops, smartphones, and tablets are a frequent-to-ubiquitous presence. (Some of the exercises would make little sense at a school that is already deliberately tech-free, or in a community where people cannot afford access to digital technology).

The exercises which accompany chapters of this book have a twofold purpose. They can be used to educate, whether in a classroom, or as parent-child activities. They are also intended for you, the reader, because refining your own screenfaring abilities is the surest foundation for cultivating the skillset in others. In order to teach kids something, *especially* deliberate use of digital technology, it is crucial to model it for them. It is not enough to say one thing and do another. Children are keen hypocrisy detectors. You need not be perfect, but you do need to make the effort.

In a group of children I worked with, whose speech seemed to consist mostly of swapping Minecraft tips, the conversation took an unexpected turn when I asked them what superpower they would most like to have. After picking their powers, they asked the question back. I said "I would like to be able to control technology. You know when people are on the bus, and they are all looking at their phones? I want to turn their phones off and see what happens."

To my astonishment, they were *excited* about the idea of turning off devices. *All* of them were. "My mom is on her phone *all the time*," one child lamented. "Mine too. She says she is working but I see her scrolling through Instagram," another agreed. "Sometimes I really want a hug," said a third "but my parents are too busy with their computers to pay attention to me."

Every child in the group shared this experience.[1] Their words gave me hope. Even though they have never known a time before tech insinuated itself between parents and children, they still know something is wrong with this picture. But they are less equipped to deal with the problem than we are. We can help them become equipped—if we walk the talk.

A Piece of the Puzzle

This book is not intended to address all issues with digital technologies, but rather to fill a gap in available resources. Many digital-age issues are already fairly widely recognised and addressed in schools: for example, misinformation, cyberbullying, internet predators, internet privacy, eye damage, and physical health. Much has been written about these topics already. The resource list at the end of this book (page 123) includes a few pointers, though it is by no means comprehensive.

Screenfarers' aim, of nurturing awareness and self-control, will indirectly contribute to many of these other issues. Children and youth who pay attention to how 'screen time' affects them and work to self-regulate will be less likely to damage their eyes by staring at screens no matter how dry and sore their eyes get, and more likely to go get healthy exercise. If they understand why so many online platforms are *designed* to keep them on screens indefinitely, then they are more likely to take measures to protect their privacy and avoid tracking. The habit-forming qualities of so many apps, games, and websites play a huge role in exacerbating all of the other internet related issues. *Screenfarers* tackles this root cause, which will help on many fronts.

The puzzle is even bigger than these other digital tech concerns, however. If we wish to address issues created by the infiltration of digital tech into every part of modern life, we must extend our consideration beyond the digital. The information and exercises in this book should be supplemented with other forms of learning: encounters with the natural world, crafts and making things, arts, hands-on science, and activities which are already staples in schools such as reading, writing, physical exercise, and so on. There are many resources out there for such activities; a few are included in the resource list.

Analog activities are important for two reasons. First, because digital technologies can become a young person's entire world. It is now possible to experience almost nothing *other* than video games, internet browsing, social media, and so on. It is easy to see how children may wish to spend all their time in digital realms if they have no other interests, and little exposure to non-digital activities. To address excessive habitual use of digital tech, it is necessary for students to have things they are excited to do that are not on a screen.

Second, non-digital activities are a venue for the human connection, learning, and skills that can be missed in favour of hours and hours on screens. By encouraging children and youth to develop non-digital interests and relationships, we can mitigate both harmful habits that digital technologies can create, *and* the loss of skills, experiences, and connections that devices can replace.

Creative, hands-on, and outdoor experiences can provide students with a sense of the wonder and potential that exists in the tangible world. They also can lead to a sense of competence in navigating this world. As a teenager, I had intelligent peers who somehow had close to zero ability to figure out simple physical tasks, such as how to turn a wingnut. This level of incompetence is very hard to overcome as a teen or adult. So many foundational skills and experiences are missing. Yet children growing up now live far more digitized lives, from a far younger age, than my generation (now in our 20s). According to a US-based report, half of two-to-four-year-olds have their own tablet or smartphone.[2] Even before COVID-19, children between the ages of zero and eight spent an average of 40 minutes a day watching videos online.[3] My mother's primary school students dream of becoming YouTube stars. One third-grader's life goal is to get one thousand 'likes' on a video. As I write this, COVID-19 is still at large— for many students, even *school* ends up squeezed through a device of one kind or another.

If a young person has no sense of competence in analog activities, no aspirations outside of the digital realm, and no sense of value beyond it, it is no wonder they might cling to an iPad as if the world would end if it were taken away. It would. But only if their world does not extend beyond the glowing rectangle.

Many argue that companies which intentionally create addictive interfaces should be held accountable for the impacts, and we should not place the responsibility for addictive tech use on the people who get caught up in it. Digital technology is required for so many essential tasks these days, and many aspects of it are rigged to encourage habitual distraction. It is not your fault, or mine, that this is the case.

But it is a mistake to place all eggs in the basket of 'regulate Silicon Valley.' Such regulation is worth attempting but extremely difficult. It may never happen in a way that solves the problem (see Chapter 16 for more details).

It is also a mistake to completely give up personal responsibility. We are not to blame for addictive app design, but that does not mean we are powerless against it without miraculous help from governments and corporations.

Defining the Objective

While writing this book I struggled to find words that accurately convey certain ideas. I would want to say something like "the internet and also some aspects of non-networked computers," or "computers, smartphones, and tablets, when used in specific ways." Neither of these roll off the tongue. Nor does "programs, websites, and applications, with some exceptions."

It has been tricky to concisely describe the aims of this book. There is no good term for what the book is trying to achieve. There is no agreed-upon term for what it is fighting against. This is partly because we are only beginning to grapple with the issues as a society and find the language for them. It is also because the digital world is messy, entangled, and fast-changing. Clearly defined labels do not come easily.

Because of these challenges of language, I want to be clear about my intentions with the words I use. To do this, I have to explain of the nature of the problem I am trying to address.

A note on 'technology'

You may notice that I avoid using the word *technology* to refer to *digital* technology. I try to use the whole phrase, **digital technology**, or *technologies*, when possible (although I sometimes use 'digital tech' or 'tech' as a stand-in, to avoid repeating the 7-syllable phrase). This is for an important reason.

I often hear people use the word to refer to their smartphone and/or computer, saying "I'm so sick of technology," or "I'm really into technology." But I do not think it is a good idea to put a smartphone in the same category as cooking with fire, bridges, gunpowder, spaceships, cutlery, movable type, MRI machines, and the steam engine—and to then *ignore that any of those other things are in the category too*, and say things about 'technology' that apply only to the smartphone.

Technology is not one unified thing. We need to stop talking about it as if it is. This way of talking, when it becomes a way of thinking, can close off the options available to us in favour of surrender to current trends. It can become a way of giving up responsibility for our choices. As a society, we have created the technologies in question and decided to use them—we have not been steamrolled by some external force called Technology that reshaped our lives of its own accord! As a society, as communities, as individuals, we can assess how different technologies impact us and whether how we are using them squares with our priorities—but this is not likely to happen if technology is treated as a monolithic, unstoppable force.

Glossing over 'technologies' with the word 'technology' can also lead to unhelpful black-and-white thinking: to question *one* aspect of *one* technology can result in being denounced as 'anti-technology.' This, obviously, hinders important conversations about how we want technologies to shape our lives, and when the costs outweigh the benefits. We need more of those conversations right now, with nuance included, on many matters that go well beyond the subject of this book.

The problem

As mentioned, there is no good single term for the source of the issues this book tackles. *Digital technology* gets close, and I sometimes use this phrase as a stand-in. Or I may just name an example, such as Facebook, smartphones, the internet, or screens, and allow the rest to follow by implication.

When I say that digital technology is similar to the problem I am addressing, let me be clear what that means. I am not saying digital technologies, or smartphones, or even Facebook are 'bad.' Rather, digital technologies happen to be a perfect medium for a suite of psychological manipulation techniques that have grown very sophisticated in the last decade.

These techniques—further explained in Chapter 3—are employed across devices and platforms in order to make them as 'persuasive' (i.e. addictive) as possible. There is no single agreed-upon term for them. A variety of labels are used: *persuasive technology*, *captology* (Computers-As-Persuasive-Technology-ology), *persuasive design*, *habit-forming technology*, and, in technical cognitive terms, *operant conditioning*. Of these, **habit-forming technology** and **behaviour design** seem the most honest and descriptive terms.

Annoyingly, both have a broader meaning than I intend. These terms can be applied in ways that are genuinely positive, and probably ways that are not digital. I use the terms here to refer to negative, manipulative applications of these techniques, rather than the entire field.

Digital technologies are ideal for behaviour design for several reasons. They remove inconveniences and barriers between different activities (including, thanks to pocketable devices, barriers between digital and non-digital activities). They make it possible to collect detailed data on each individual. They also allow designers immense freedom to structure experience. As a medium, they allow for near-complete control of the choices available to people, and the consequences of different choices.

> The language around this topic is so convoluted that one almost wonders if those in the industry are deliberately making it hard to research or talk about the subject! Most likely, it is simply a matter of people who like to "move fast and break things" all making up their own terms (and then people who study their antics coming up with still more).
>
> Part of the language convolution seems to stem from the desire of different platforms to have their own terms for things. Various social media sites have 'feeds' and 'notifications' but sometimes the notifications are called 'alerts' or the feed is called a 'timeline.' With all these minor variations, it can be hard to see the forest for the trees (or the network for the feeds)—not to mention hard to talk about it.

Digital technologies are a great medium for psychological manipulation because of their flexibility, interconnectedness, and data-processing power: precisely the characteristics which make them so useful to us. As with seafaring, it is hard to disentangle the harms from the benefits. When does something become manipulative in a problematic sense? All digital technologies have user interfaces—all of the interactions you have with any device, application, or website are inevitably shaped by design choices which influence behaviour. Since we know a lot about how behaviour is affected by design, any time a space (a digital space, or even a building) is designed, behaviour design in some form or another is unavoidable.

The complexity of this situation is a big part of why it is so hard to address. If the only thing smartphones and laptops did was make people develop addictive behaviours with negative mental and physical health effects, it would be simple to agree to get rid of them. Obviously, this is not the case, and a more nuanced approach is needed.

The current rampant use of habit-forming techniques on digital platforms is incentivised by the financial structure of the internet. Most of the internet is powered by ad revenue—

especially services that are free of charge. As a result, *the collective aim of habit-forming techniques is to encourage people to buy more stuff.* However, the approach to this goal is circuitous. Digital platforms encourage people to spend as many hours on them as possible. The longer they are on, the more targeted ads they can be shown, and the more personal data is collected to be sold to advertisers.[4]

The net result of these habit-forming techniques is that people have less control over themselves. We are trained to act impulsively. As a result, we have difficulty focussing on tasks, remembering things, and behaving the way we intend to. Another result is increasing dependence on digital devices for basic mental skills that are the foundations for learning, creativity, and thought. As multidimensional as digital technologies are, I think we can agree that these particular impacts are detrimental to individuals, communities, and societies.

The goal

So, the problem is behaviour design that leads to thoughtless, impulsive, unintentional, passive behaviour. What can we call the opposite of this? What is the practice of becoming less manipulable, more deliberate, of becoming addiction-proof, of inserting thought back into unconscious habit-loops?

"Attention hygiene" might be a good start. "Digital wellness" is starting to catch on, but I feel like it evokes a spa experience rather than something practical, and it does not precisely capture what I am getting at. For lack of any decent term, I am calling this thing **screenfaring**.

In this book, I investigate the following problems:

- Invisibility and sneakiness of habit-forming techniques
- Habits created by aggressively habit-forming apps/platforms
- General impulsivity and lack of self-control cultivated by current digital paradigm
- Lack of barriers inherent to digital technology
- Loss of skills outsourced to devices

To address these problems, I lay out the following solutions:

- Learn about/teach about psychology of habit-forming tech and how to recognise it
- Intentionally alter habits through awareness, motivation, and practice
- Strengthen general awareness and self-control through practice
- Deliberately create helpful barriers
- Practice and value core skills that are at risk of being outsourced (and play outside!)

Part I, the core of *Screenfarers*, focusses on the habit-forming technology industry. Chapter 1 introduces an approach to developing awareness of the ways one's own mind is affected by digital experiences. Chapter 2 outlines some of the historical, cultural, and economic reasons for the extreme prevalence of habit-forming techniques in the present time and introduces ways of creating barriers which contain digital habits. Chapter 3 explains the theories and techniques underlying habit-forming interface design. Chapters 4 and 5 tackle two important gaps in the theories, each of which is a key to developing our mental immune systems. Chapter 6 discusses how and when digital aids to limiting device use can be helpful, and when they can interfere. Chapter 7 shows how the different practical strategies presented throughout Part I fit together, building many layers of resistance to undesired habit-formation.

Part II explores the other side of the habit-forming technology coin: the habits and mental skills that may atrophy (or never be formed in the first place) when we outsource key mental capacities to devices. Chapter 8 describes this process in general, and extends the framework introduced in Part I which helps make the effects easy to see in oneself. Chapters 9-12 go into more detail on the specifics: attention/perception, imagination, thought, memory, and empathy/human connection. Each of these chapters includes exercises for developing the threatened mental skill in question; as well as information on how each skill works, why it matters, and an inspiring example of what human minds are capable of in each domain. Chapter 13 takes a step back, delving into why we act as though outsourcing mental skills is inevitable, whether it actually *is* inevitable, and what is at stake when we allow devices to replace the abilities discussed throughout Part II.

Part III contains some suggestions for teaching screenfaring and awareness of habit-forming design. Chapter 14 describes the variety of ways someone can be a skilled screenfarer and brings up a few cautionary points around how assessment could interfere with students developing screenfaring skills, if mishandled. Chapter 15 highlights the importance of parent-teacher collaboration and describes some of the steps parents and teachers can take to create favourable conditions for deliberate digital tech use to develop. Chapter 16 gathers together many of the big questions that arise from the topic of persuasive technology—ethical, legal, social, philosophical. These issues are touched on throughout the book, and Chapter 16 collects them in one place (with some additional topics and resources) for use in classroom discussions and inquiry activities. Chapter 17 describes my hopes for subsequent editions, how an educational response to the problem of persuasive technology might develop in the future, and how you can contribute to such a movement.

Part I is the most important section of the book. If you are in a hurry to tackle these issues you may wish to jump to Part III after reading Part I, and return to Part II later.

Part I: Habit-Forming Technologies

1. Seeing What Is Hidden in Plain Sight

Primary and secondary school students learn about outer space, distant geographies, ancient history, and microscopic atoms. Meanwhile, they often spend hours per day on smartphones, computers, and game consoles. If they have been taught anything about these daily features of their lives, it is that too much screen time may be bad for them in some vague way, or perhaps some programming skills. They are not taught the ways that their devices are literally attempting to 'program' *them*.

To set the stage for this chapter, I'd like you to do a short experiment (seriously—pause your reading for a moment and really do it). First, open whatever social media or email accounts you have and look at the unread emails or notifications. Don't click on them to read or follow up, or scroll through any feeds. Instead, stop. Close all the browser windows, and jot down some observations:

- How did it make you feel to see the notifications/new emails? To not click on them? To close the windows? Describe.
- What is the origin of this feeling? Why do you feel this way?
- Take your explanation and keep asking why. See how far you can dig. For example: *I did not want to close the window because I really wanted to read the top email in my inbox, and my heart started racing a little just seeing it. Why? It looked like something important which needed immediate response. Why? Because it's from Charlie, who only contacts me for important things.*
- Was your feeling useful? Did it correspond accurately with the importance/urgency of what you were seeing?

In a society that prides itself on scientific knowledge and availability of information, it is incredible how little we appear to know about the effects of digital technologies on the mind. This matter is central to the daily experience of billions of people. Whatever the effects are, they have defined the lives of entire generations globally. Yet they are largely treated as a mystery.

As more attention is drawn to issues around digital technology, a heated controversy has emerged over what the science says on the issue of 'screen time' and kids. Some are sounding alarms; others denounce such alarms as a 'moral panic' and point to research that shows benefits of technology use, or at least no clear sign of harms.

There are several reasons for the controversy. One is the nature of what the studies (and particular kinds of studies) can and cannot tell us about the effects of digital technology use.

Different uses of technology have different mental effects, and studies do not often effectively separate these.[1] To compound the issue, two people could be exhibiting exactly the same outer behaviour, but have a different process happening inside them which alters how they will be affected. Say, both are browsing Facebook, but one has a clear purpose while the other is aimlessly poking around. This type of nuance is very hard to include in research.

Another source of controversy is disagreement over values, which actually has nothing to do with the science. Even if we had perfect knowledge of how various interactions with digital technologies affect the full variety of people, we might still not agree on whether more internet use or smartphone use is 'good' for kids or 'bad' for them. These interactions, like all our interactions, are how we construct ourselves; children, in particular, are in the crucial early stages of that construction. There is no one 'correct' answer to the question of how human beings should construct themselves. Myriad societies have wildly different answers to this question; within each society, so too can communities and individuals. Is it more important for

The word 'science' and its sub-categories are much abused in the media, popular culture, and by various institutions, as an invocation of The Ultimate Authority. Sometimes it gets to the point where information degenerates into a game of Science Says:

> *Science says, clap your hands. Science says… touch your nose.*
> *Science says… stand on one foot. Now stomp your feet. Hah! Science didn't sa-ay!*

This can make it hard to have a reasonable conversation about the impacts of technologies. When a study is published that could be loosely interpreted as meaning 'tech is good for kids,' a bunch of journalists will take it and run with it, dropping any nuance or awareness of limitations on the way. When a study links tech use with suicidality or anxiety or learning impairment, the same oversimplification can happen. To make matters worse, the vast majority of these studies only show correlation (kids who play more hours of video games also have a shorter attention spans) not causation (did a short attention span make them more likely to play video games, or did the video games shorten their attention span—or both?), a crucial distinction often ignored in media portrayals.

Knowledge of the dangers of Science Says is key for navigating the present world in an informed manner, the subject of the psychology of digital tech very much included. This topic can be a good opportunity to get students thinking what exactly science is, and to help them tease out some of the nuance.

Science can refer to a lot of things: an institution, a body of cumulative knowledge, a method or collection of methods. Some use the word as verbal seasoning, to spice up their claims and sound more knowledgeable. Some use it to describe belief in the infallibility of scientists; on the other hand, Nobel-Prize-winning physicist Richard Feynman defines science as "the belief in the ignorance of experts" (Feynman, 187).

Have students ask: what kind of 'science' are we talking about here? The subject of habit-forming technology is a good opportunity to delve into how the scientific method works, when it doesn't, and issues such as cherry-picking the evidence, replicability, cognitive biases, and funding from organizations that have a stake in the results.

children to grow up proficient in coding or with the ability to pick up on in-person social nuance? A choice one way or the other will have huge impacts in many domains of life, but the choice largely depends on cultural priorities, not experimental evidence.

There is a way past the controversy: we must stop treating 'screen time' as a single uniform thing. Even dividing it up into video games, database research, Netflix, Pinterest is too crude. The effects of digital technology involve interaction between the platform, the person using it, their state of mind, and other contents of their mind, experience, and life.

Understanding the inner workings of one's own mind has many benefits beyond contributing to a healthier relationship with the digital world. It involves learning how to learn, an ability which obviously produces very effective learners!

This may sound complicated. It certainly is complicated to research, generalize about, or make snappy headlines about. But it can be simply a matter of paying attention. The best scientific instrument we have for observing what is happening in our minds is our minds themselves. Introspection provides insight customized to your *particular* mind, which is more useful than generalizing statistics (which can fail to even say something general).

Through practices that develop awareness, we can distinguish different ways digital technologies affect us. This awareness not only informs—it also provides an opportunity for action. If you can see how you are being shaped by digital technologies, you can change your behaviour to remove harms and increase benefits, whatever that means to you. The same is true for any young person.

Even awareness alone has an impact on the effects of digital tech. Many of the most clearly harmful effects of digital technologies come from unconscious or semi-conscious habits they encourage—passive use, binge-watching, sleep disruption, sedentary lifestyles. The first step to intentionally changing such habits is to bring them to conscious awareness.

The simplest way to think about habits, and by extension the ways digital technologies shape your mind, is this:

Everything you do is practice.

Many animals adapt to their environments through learning and practice. Humans, however, take it a step further: we have the incredible ability to choose what we want to become, and transform ourselves into it through practice.

There are things we do (such as circulate blood) which are not learned or habitual. And, of course, there are limits to how practice can transform us. Our brains (and bodies) have limitations. There are certain limits on working memory, for example, and humans tend to be bad at multitasking. Practice cannot necessarily remove these limitations, though it can make us better at working within and around them. *Everything you do is practice* is not a precise fact—it is a useful simplification that illuminates many of the mental effects of digital technologies.

Such effects can be largely explained either by what you are encouraged to practice (e.g. constant attention shifts, clicking before thinking, a certain kind of 'flow state' which takes you down a rabbit-hole), or what you neglect to practice (e.g. remembering information, deliberate action, social skills, emotional self-regulation).

This varies between people, of course. One person might practice feeling self-conscious and ashamed due to seeing so many photos of models on Instagram. Another might practice picking political arguments in YouTube comments, reading food-related clickbait articles, and Googling questions about quantum physics when feeling anxious about relationship issues. Can you imagine a standardized questionnaire or brain scan which can tease out all of these possibilities? For every single person who is concerned about how they use digital technology? This is where personal observation and self-awareness comes in.

Video games are sometimes lauded for improving hand-eye co-ordination (thumb-eye may be more accurate). But the tests of co-ordination are often basically video games. The studies may therefore show that playing video games makes you better at playing video games.

Hand-eye co-ordination has to be calibrated differently in the physical world, and that involves far more complexity than any virtual environment—not to mention co-ordination of more body parts. When someone who plays video games all day tries to walk on a slightly uneven trail and trips all over the place, you start to see how much their 'co-ordination' is worth outside of the virtual world.

What are you practicing?

Exercises: Links

Neurons in the human brain organise themselves by forming connections. As we learn and acquire habits, one thing becomes linked to another. These links are also described as 'pathways,' and you do not need to be a neuroscientist to notice them or experience their formation. Anytime you practice something, and it gets easier with practice, you are forming pathways. You can read these words because sound-combinations in the English language have been linked in your brain with meanings, and groups of letters have been linked with those words. Links and pathways are the stuff habits are made of.

Habit-forming technologies exploit this characteristic of our minds. They are designed to create particular chains of linkage and association, pathways which generate revenue by keeping people on their devices. The first step towards cultivating a deliberate relationship with the digital world is to practice noticing these linkages and chains—both in your own mind, and in digital interfaces. Each of the following exercises develops different aspects of this awareness.

Focus Challenge

Choose a productive task you need to accomplish (one which requires computer use).

Then, as you did at the beginning of this chapter, open social media and/or email accounts and look at notifications, *without* clicking on them to read or follow up.

This time, however, set a timer five, ten, or twenty minutes, and try to accomplish the task you originally chose.

Can you do it, without being tempted to find out what your messages say? Without responding to any new dings and buzzes your computer or phone throws at you?

After the timer ends, write some reflections:

- What feelings did you have? What things made you feel that way?
- Did you end up looking at emails or notifications anyways?
- Did you have strategies to avoid looking at them? Closing the windows? Hiding them from yourself?
- Did you make progress on the task you set out to do?

Further reflection questions:

- Are you satisfied with how you relate to the internet?
- With your level of focus?
- What do you think could improve?
- What did you learn from this?
- What strategies might help you manage attention?
- What would you like to learn more about?

This challenge can be repeated later and compared with the earlier results, to assess growth and change. It can also be used as a regular practice, for building attention-control muscles. And after learning new anti-distraction strategies, you can use this exercise to test them out and help integrate them into existing habits.

Design Detective

Open a website or internet platform you use frequently (social media and news websites are particularly good for this exercise).

On a sheet of paper, sketch the visual layout of the site. This need not be a detailed drawing. It can be as simple as labelled boxes of what is where (for a news website, you could have a box to represent a list of headlines in the sidebar).

Notice where the website draws your eye. What does it invite you to do? On your diagram, label the design features, icons, and phrases that stand out most. Jot down a few notes on what makes them stand out, and what the intention behind them might be. Some things to keep in mind for each feature:

- Appearance: colour, contrast, shape, size, placement, relation to other elements, movement, etc.
- Significance: what does it mean? What does it make you think of? How does it make you feel?

- Behaviour: what action does it encourage you to take?

When you have labelled the diagram, write answers to the following questions:

- Based on the design, what do you think the website designer most wants you to do? What actions seem prioritized?
- Are there things you might want to do which are not included in your options? What options are omitted?
- Are there actions you can take that are possible, yet discouraged by the design? Why might they be discouraged?
- How does the intention underlying the design, as you perceive it, compare to your intention in using the website? What aspects overlap? What aspects are different? (This could be depicted visually as a Venn Diagram).
- Why would the designer's intentions overlap with yours in the way they do? Why would they not overlap in other places?
- What do you think the purpose of the website is, from the perspective of the company behind it?

This activity could be expanded on in a classroom setting by having students compare their findings, looking for patterns. Looking at the same site allows them to compare their perceptions to those of others. Not only may different people make different observations of the same site, in some cases the same site will present itself differently to different people. Investigating different websites will start to reveal commonalities. This will help extend awareness of design to digital experience in general. The benefits of both these approaches can be combined by having two or three students look at each website, and several different websites examined by the class. The students looking at the same site can compare with each other first, and then discuss in groups where everyone looked at something different. A few cross-comparison questions:

- Are there behaviours that multiple websites prompt you to do? What are they? Which websites encourage them? Why might this be?
- Underlying the encouraged behaviours are the overall goals behind the website. Based on your guesses of these intentions, are there particular intentions which underlie the design of multiple websites? Are there any that are common to all of the ones the class examined? Do any other patterns emerge?
- Are there different amounts of overlap on different sites between one's intention using the site and the inferred intention of the site design? Why might particular sites overlap more or less?
- How do different websites draw your attention to things? Do they use some of the same techniques?

'Design Detective' can be one way of introducing the subject of behaviour design. As a reader of this book, you likely have some answers to the 'why' questions above. But asking these questions to students who may not know anything about the subject helps get them paying attention to what they see online. They may never have thought about the matter, yet they may become curious as they notice how intentional design underlies their experience.

Screenfarer's Log: Tracking Digital Habits

For a week, record your own ordinary use of digital technologies (at this point, don't worry about changing anything—just observe):

- Write down a start time and finish time every time you use a mobile phone, computer, tablet, watch television, etc.
- Add up the total number of hours and minutes at the end of each day, and the total number in the week.

If you find yourself using a device frequently but briefly—for example, frequently pulling out a smartphone to check the time—this can be tracked by simply keeping a tally and estimating how much time each mark on the tally represents (in the example, maybe 5 seconds). It may be worth having a separate tally for how many times you *touch* your phone (as opposed to how many times you use it for something): on average, American participants in a recent study used their phones 76 times per day, and touched their phones 2617 times per day.[2]

There are programs which will help you track your use of digital technologies, and these have their place. But there are also benefits to doing it yourself, especially at first. Keeping track of your own usage helps create the habit of directing attention to your habits. It also makes whatever you find out more meaningful than simply being told by an app.

Mapping a Path to Distraction

Zooming in on exactly *how* you get distracted makes it easier to stop a distraction in its tracks, before it happens. In tracking your digital habits, have you noticed any particular situations or kinds of content that repeatedly lead you astray from your intended task?

Pick one of these, and try to map out (visually or in writing) the sequence of actions you take from beginning to end. Include things you perceive, actions you take, and the thought process that accompanies both of these. What emotions or thoughts underlie your actions? How do you justify them to yourself?

For example, I noticed that I frequently get distracted by reading blogs. As I looked closer at this, I realised that it follows a pattern. It starts when I am already on my computer, but I am either trying to avoid a difficult task, or not sure what to do with myself. I will then visit different blogs that I follow, to see if anything new has been posted. If I find a new post, I read it, although that was not originally part of the plan. I generally keep scrolling and read the comments as well. There are always links in the comments to articles elsewhere—I often read those, too. It is tricky to stop myself reading the comments because of the 'fear of missing out:' they have pointed me to so many interesting things before. But reading them can also result in hours and hours of not doing whatever difficult but important task I was trying to avoid in the first place.

Having investigated how this chain of distraction unfolds, I now notice it before it happens: as soon as I feel a desire to procrastinate and think about looking at a blog, I catch myself and consider whether I can afford to spend three hours on that at the moment. Awareness of where the first action leads brushes aside justifications like 'I'll just read one little thing' or 'I'll just check if there's anything new and not read it' (followed by reading it). When I want to go read a blog, I can now tell the difference between using it to avoid something and seeking it out because I have time and want to read it.

If catching the habit before it happens is not enough to evade distraction, understanding the whole sequence also reveals other ways to disrupt it. For example, in my case, I can decide to not look at any of the blogs I frequent for a month. Or, before starting to read a post, decide that I will not look at any of the comments.

See what happens when you map out one of your paths to distraction. How does it change the habit?

Simply by paying careful attention to digital experience, observing both what happens on the screen and what happens in your mind, it would be possible to rediscover much of the theoretical content of this book. However, the historical trends from which habit-forming technologies emerged have another story to tell us. By examining the past, we can learn how the current digital paradigm became so aggressively psychologized, why, and what we can do as individuals to avoid the worst of it while still benefiting from the best.

2. The Fertile Ground for Mind Control

The history of persuasive technology is, in a sense, history itself. People have been trying to control each other in various ways, subtle or not-so-subtle, pretty much forever. Everything from legal systems to temple architecture, poetry, government, war, and manners can be seen as an attempt to shape the behaviour of others. There have always been various forms of coercion, persuasion, punishment, and incentive bubbling around in humanity's repertoire. That is not necessarily a bad thing.

A few centuries ago, something new started to happen. Techniques began to emerge to persuade people to *consume*. Not to pay taxes or go to church; not to follow the law or enlist in the army. Not to *buy my merchandise, instead of that other stuff.* This new sort of persuasion encouraged people to *buy more, in general.* To develop new wants that, through social pressure, became new needs.

This chapter is a brief overview of how human beings have been deliberately molded into consumers. This historical trend provides important context for making sense of the present character of digital experiences. The art and science of encouraging to buy more has always been entwined with technical innovation and communications media, as well as political, economic, and cultural circumstance. We are where we are today as a result of the interactions of those particular circumstances.

> The contents of this chapter could be used to link the topic of habit-forming technology to pretty much any school subject: psychology, technology, media studies, politics, economics, math, literature...

Industrialization and the Twin Efficiencies

The factories of the Industrial Revolution were incredibly efficient at producing goods in very little time, thanks to innovations in steam power, mechanization, and division of labour. This is a well-known bit of history. What gets less attention is where all those efficiently produced goods went.

After all, the slower handcrafts of pre-industrial times were generally sufficient to keep people clothed and provide for their needs. There were exceptions to this in periods of famine and shortage, but industrialization did not exactly end poverty or starvation. Human needs were more-or-less the same as before. People were working as hard as ever (or harder). Yet production was hundreds or even thousands of times faster. Where was all this stuff going?

With efficient production came lowered costs and a need for newly efficient forms of retail, to sell the mountains of inexpensive goods churned out by factories. Shopping had been a slow process in the 1700s. To buy a pair of shoes, for instance, you went to a shoemaker's workshop: a shop in both senses of the word. You probably had the shoes custom made for you, and spent a while haggling over the price. All this took a lot of time.

In the early 1800s, people began to sell things in new ways. Fixed prices removed the haggling. Standard clothing sizes removed the customization. And many different kinds of products started to be sold under one roof, in ever-larger buildings.

But it was not enough to simply make purchasing easier. If people stopped purchasing when they had what they needed, or even when they had what they already wanted, the factories would soon cease to be profitable. To fund and justify continued industry, people had to be encouraged to buy more. Printed advertising—posters, flyers, newspaper and magazine ads— was one way to do this. Fashion trends set by the wealthy also contributed. But a powerful new approach emerged, in the form of architecture (the original choice architecture). *Le Bon Marché* in Paris was the first building designed and built for the purpose of shaping people into consumers.

The *Marché* had originally been haberdashery, a small store for sewing supplies. Over the decades, the owners gradually added other kinds of products. Eventually, there were numerous departments carrying everything from the new "ready-to-wear" fashion lines to umbrellas, toys, cutlery, furniture, scissors, perfume and horse tack.[3] The store slowly bought up adjacent buildings, expanding until it had control of the whole block.

This enabled it to be completely rebuilt in 1869, filling the entire block. This time, it was no ordinary building. It looked like a palace, a theatre, a cathedral. The intention of this grandeur was to intrigue customers. To dazzle them, invite them to linger, and inspire a culture of novelty and luxury. On each of its street corners, the *Marché* product display windows bulged outwards, glass rotundas calculated to maximize view angles from the street. Doors were placed to encourage circulation and browsing, and a sweeping gilded staircase was built to draw people to the upper floors.[4] It was the first building designed to shape behaviour with the purpose of encouraging people to buy more stuff, and it is still doing so in Paris today.

The design process behind *Le Bon Marché* is analogous to modern website design. If you consider the paragraph above, you will find many familiar parallels on the internet. The same intentions have simply been applied to hyperlinked two-dimensional screen-space, instead of three-dimensional architectural space.

The *Bon Marché* model spread to England and America and beyond, evolving into today's shopping malls. Industrialization had mechanized work, making it hyper-efficient. The other half of the production-consumption equation was solved by enterprises like the *Marché*, which intentionally cultivated a culture where shopping became both more convenient and a prime leisure activity. This, in turn, supported industrial production. The factories made previously undreamt-of material riches accessible to the masses. Yet the masses could not be allowed to be satisfied with their riches, lest the factories lose their market.

Increase in material consumption had already been happening through global trade networks, even before industrial production—but industrialization shifted it into an entirely new gear. This was not without its benefits; it led to great leaps in human knowledge and a proliferation of new choices for individuals. Luxuries that had previously been restricted to the wealthiest few became widely affordable. I do not have space here for balanced consideration of all the varied impacts of industrial development. What is key for our purposes is that highly efficient, large scale industry made it essential to encourage, persuade, pressure, even train people to buy more. One efficiency required another.

Consumerization and the Mind-Molding Machine

"Our enormously productive economy demands that we make consumption our way of life, that we convert the buying and use of goods into rituals...We require not only 'forced draft' consumption, but 'expensive' consumption as well. We need things consumed, burned up, worn out, replaced, and discarded at an ever increasing pace...the total effect of all the advertising and promotion and selling is to create and maintain the multiplicity and intensity of wants that are the spur to the standard of living in the United States...the whole problem of molding the American mind is involved here."

~Victor Lebow, 1955 [5]

Following the tradition of the late 1800s, American industrial manufacturers of the 1920s were concerned about "need saturation"—about people becoming satisfied with what they had. They set out to increase consumption to match production. The explicit goal was to create new dissatisfactions, needs, and wants, largely using marketing.

It was hard to overcome the stubborn frugality of American culture. Slowly, people began to develop new tastes and embrace more consumption-heavy lifestyles. Then, that gradual shift suddenly reversed: in 1929, the stock market collapsed, and the Great Depression made frugality a necessity.

The Depression was followed by the Second World War. The USA ramped up its manufacturing capacity to produce tanks, artillery, and other equipment and supplies for the war effort. When the war was over, all this investment in manufacturing had to be put to use somehow. Once again, manufacturers were keen to see production power balanced out by consumption.

This time, after a decade of economic depression followed by wartime scarcity and rations, people were happy to buy all kinds of new products. Consumption was even transformed into an explicit ideal: the consumer was encouraged to spend for the prosperity of the country. The quote from Victor Lebow above is not criticism—it is advocacy.

A major difference between the '50s push for consumption and the '20s push was the prevalence of television. The first TV ad was placed in 1941.[6] Since the '50s, the proportion of the US GDP spent on advertising has increased exponentially. Until the internet came along, television advertising accounted for the vast majority of this spending.

Advertising existed before TV, of course, from the ads produced by the in-house printing press of *Le Bon Marché,* to the radio ads of the '30s, magazine ads of the 1700s, to many varieties of signage and street hawking going back to antiquity. But television rapidly overtook other forms of advertising because it was vastly more effective. In the same 1955 journal article which is quoted at start of this chapter, Victor Lebow praises the medium:

> *"Probably the most powerful weapon of the dominant producers lies in their use of television…television achieves three results to an extent no other advertising medium has ever approached. First, it creates a captive audience. Second, it submits that audience to the most intensive indoctrination. Third, it operates on the entire family."*

In the earliest days of television, it was a communal activity—neighbours would crowd around a single TV to watch shows. As more people acquired TV sets it became increasingly isolating. First there was one per household, shared by the family. Then multiple sets per household became common: by the 1990s three quarters of households in the US had more than one TV. [7]

Arguments in support of democracy, the competitive market, and even social justice movements are often predicated on the idea that we can make the world a better place by giving people what they want.

But if it is possible for marketers to create wants or even needs in a population, then what? (If making people need new things sounds like it is beyond the power of persuasive technologies, consider how easy it would be to have a job or social life without access to a computer or cellphone right now).

What if a few CEOs get to largely control the tools that can influence what people want? Every aspect of our social, emotional, economic, material, and political lives is profoundly shaped by the pervasiveness of techniques of persuasion. Is this inevitable? Is it good? Are there other options?

In his book *Bowling Alone: The Collapse and Revival of American Community,* Robert Putnam examines the steep decline in social connectedness in America over the latter half of the 20th century. He analyzes the available social data to determine why this deterioration of human relationships and community occurred.

Nearly all factors Putnam identifies as reasons for decline in community are related to television or to increasing industrialization and consumption. Television ate up leisure time, and replaced activities that bring people into contact with each other. Suburban sprawl and long commutes, enabled by the material wealth of industrial manufacture and the cars it produces, broke up the social structure of neighbourhoods. Pressures of time and money were created when women entered the workforce: with families supported on two incomes instead of one, employers were able to lower wages until two incomes were *required* for many, not optional. This unraveled the fabric of many communities, as most women no longer had time to organize the social activities which had previously maintained it (at the same time, more workers enabled more industrial production). The other major factor Putnam links to the decline in community is shifts in values across different generations. He suspects these changes are at least partly tied to the influence of television.

Putnam quotes T.S. Eliot: "[television] is a medium of entertainment which permits millions of people to listen to the same joke at the same time, and yet remain lonesome." [8] He also notes that human beings suffer when they are lonely—not only mentally and emotionally, but in their physical health: people with higher social connectedness are less likely to experience colds, heart attacks, strokes and cancer. And, of course, they tend to be happier with higher life satisfaction, while loneliness is highly related to depression.

I do not mean to imply that only negative things have come from the latter half of the 20th century, the effects of television on society, or even the effects of advertising. The complexity of these topics is beyond this chapter. I simply wish to show, in brief, some of the historic foundations for why digital media took on the more pernicious aspects of its present form.

Much of the groundwork for the habit-forming technologies that shape our society today was laid before the internet existed in any form. Industries dependent on continued growth in consumption levels were expanding, which provided motivation for aggressive use of psychology to sell products. At the same time, the social fabric disintegrated as men and women poured more and more time into work and television. The resulting culture of loneliness likely increased the vulnerability of many people to marketing techniques which symbolically promised them happiness, friendship, love, and approval.

Television viewing also, as Putnam observes, became increasingly habitual and less intentional over time.[9] This pattern of media consumption may have further helped lay psychological foundations for habitual use of digital technologies.

The allure of digital technologies partly depends on what other options are apparent: for a child whose options are watching TV or exploring the internet and playing videogames, the interactive options may seem far more engaging. If the choice is between staring at a little screen and running around in the woods with friends, it is less clear that digital technologies are more engaging. They may instead be treated as useful tools for certain tasks.

The effects of a technology are not independent of its context. Imagine that you somehow inserted smartphone technology into the Roman Empire, or pre-contact Aboriginal Australia, or the Ming Dynasty, or even early 20th century. The devices would certainly not be used in exactly the same ways as they are now. Nor would they have identical psychological effects. People might decide they are boring toys and toss them out. Or they might find uses for them that would never occur to us. The ways digital technologies affect us have emerged out of the unfolding of history, and they cannot be fully understood apart from it.

Digitalization in Context

In a world saturated with the passive entertainment of television, digital technologies made a splash. Now, everyone could *participate*. No longer simply viewers, internet users were bestowed with agency. Anyone could create content, adding a social dimension to the new medium.[10]

This did not happen right away. Computers of the '60s were huge mainframes that filled entire rooms. Back then, there were no keyboards or screens. A computer program was a stack of cards with holes punched in them. They resembled the punch card 'programs' of the Jacquard loom, which had enabled woven patterns to be automated during the Industrial Revolution.[11]

Operating these early computers was a technical skill, perhaps more similar to the loom than to what we think of as computers today. The early internet was a tool of academics, funded by the US military. Its rise to ubiquity, and the computer's transformation from the industrial-scale mainframe into the personal computer, took decades of interface innovations, technical refinement, and price reduction. Before digital technology could enter widespread use, it had to become small, interactive, and cheap.[12]

Personal computing may have become cheap, but the internet as a whole is very expensive. In the age of wi-fi and smartphone data, the networks can seem intangible. But they cannot exist without a physical infrastructure of ocean-spanning fiber optic cables, cell towers, enormous data processing banks, and teams of sleepless programmers.

We who use the internet generally do not pay for all this directly. It is not covered by fees to internet service providers. Computer technologies make content distribution incredibly cheap, so it is not covered by paying for content either. Cheap distribution, in combination with attempts to undercut the price of the competition and the rise of user-created content, has resulted in the proliferation of free content and services online. Many people now expect these things to be free as a matter of course.

Facebook's ad revenue for the 3rd quarter of 2020 (Jul, Aug, and Sept) was **$21.2 billion.** There were **2.74 billion people** using Facebook at least once a month in this time, and **1.82 billion** using the platform daily.

A rough average cost for Facebook ads is **$0.50/click**, and **$10/1000 views** ('impressions'). About **0.9%** of people who see an ad on Facebook click on it.

How many ad 'impressions' per quarter would it take to generate Facebook's ad revenue? How many clicks would it take? How many, per person, per day, on average? What if you only count daily users? If 0.9% of people who see an ad click it, how many clicks and views per person per day?

If you use Facebook, how much do you think they've made off your activity in the last week? Over the course of your life?

See Ch. 16 for sources and more detail.

But cheap distribution does not mean it was cheap to produce in the first place—the money has to come from somewhere. Much of the funding for the internet comes from advertising, and from selling personal data to advertisers. This personal data, and the time we spend looking at ads, is the price of most 'free' content—an arrangement often referred to as the **attention economy**.

Other monetization strategies coexist with the attention economy. Some platforms, for example, provide limited free service which is supported by paid premium subscriptions. However, the combination of data collection and advertising is extremely widespread. And it is the basis for terrifyingly large and powerful tech companies like Google and Facebook.

Selling ad space is nothing new—this strategy has funded many a print magazine since the 1700s, not to mention its use in newspapers, radio shows, and television. But the digital attention economy enables new psychological tricks. Older forms of advertising could encourage viewers or listeners to form mental associations between a product and positive things or desires they might have. But, as the next chapter will explain, digital technologies make it possible to directly train users to take *actions* that companies desire. Digital interfaces can guide users through the motions of forming habits, gently controlling ('designing') their behaviour—without them even noticing. The effects of this strategy are heightened by how digital technology makes it easy to collect detailed information about each user. They can target each individual with behavioural cues (and ads) based on that personal data.

Habit-forming techniques are relentlessly employed by companies who need to turn a profit in the new 'free' paradigm. For digital platforms in the attention economy, the bottom line depends on maximising the time users spend on devices. Netflix CEO Reed Hastings even claimed that his company's number one competitor was not other companies, it was *sleep*: "we're competing with sleep on the margin. And so, it's a very large pool of time." [13]

This would be troubling enough if it were only affecting adults. However, children of all ages are also targeted by habit-forming technologies, and it is increasingly common that they have devices of their own.

In his book *Indistractable*, Nir Eyal (whose work will be discussed further in Chapter 3) makes an important point about children's motivations. According to Self Determination Theory, a widely accepted psychological framework, all people seek competence, autonomy, and connection with others. Eyal argues that today's children have their autonomy more heavily restricted than ever, in the name of safety—even though they are growing up in a world that is safer than ever (at least in wealthy countries). An unending stream of horrific news is delivered to us, which can distort our perceptions of real dangers. Out of caution, our present society gives children few opportunities for competence, autonomy, and connection. Gone are the days when it was normal for children to roam the woods and streets on their own. Between packed schedules and constant supervision, digital devices are sometimes the only place for them to feel skilled, have a sense of freedom, and connect with friends. [14]

It is not a bad thing that children and youth use digital technologies for these purposes, but it is certainly a shame for them to have no other options. I remember how much my sense of freedom and my connection with others depended on my laptop in my early teens. I would have been quite happy for those things to come in other forms. But, in a hyper-cautious environment, with a teen culture that took place on social media, there were few options.

Parenting which allows children more responsibility for themselves and autonomy in the physical world helps address such needs. With non-digital venues for autonomy, competence, and connection, children would have less reason to cling to their devices. After all, while virtual content is often described as extremely "stimulating," it can be far less stimulating than the 3D, surround-sound, full-sensory experience of the real world!

Behaviour designers are not entirely to blame for our pervasive over-use of digital devices. Wittingly or unwittingly, they are exploiting elements of contemporary society which contribute to unhealthy habit formation. Their designs are alluring in the context of a society trained in 'rituals of consumption' for the last two hundred years. A society accustomed to passive entertainment by the television, and increasingly devoid of community. A society where children are kept indoors, sometimes so safe that safety itself becomes a danger to their health. Designers' efforts to encourage more 'time on device,' ad clicks, and impulse buys are part of a larger, evolving, social, cultural, and economic structure set in motion by the gears of the industrial revolution.

Exercises: Barriers

The architects of the online experience have, paradoxically, managed to turn the active participation that made the internet so special in the first place into a new form of passivity. The condition which enables this is the nature of digital technologies, which I mentioned in the introduction: they allow barriers between activities to be removed.

In the physical world, various inconveniences and preparations separate one activity from another. To cook, one must get out the ingredients and utensils. To read a book, one must take it off the shelf and open it up. To go to work, one must get dressed and travel there (or at least put on a shirt and open Zoom...).

But in the digital world, everything is a click or two away: one's work or study tasks are a click away from cat videos, Facebook, email, projects, games, music, blogs, ebooks, communication with friends around the world—the whole circus of the internet and the entire toolkit of the modern computer. A smartphone takes this convenience even further, ensuring that all these possibilities are just a few taps away from every moment, no matter where you go (if you choose to take it along).

This ease is empowering, in some respects. But it can make it hard to focus, creating habits of distraction. The trouble with such convenient, malleable multitools is that the only thing keeping their many different uses separate from each other is our own habits of discipline and willpower. That's the only barrier between work and entertainment. Without the inconveniences that bookend separate activities in the physical world, different activities can bleed into each other. And habits of distraction formed in the digital world can creep into all other corners of life.[15]

A "tech fast" or "digital detox" refers to a hiatus from digital technology, whether for a day, a week, or a month. This approach is sometimes dismissed as an unfeasible solution to problems of the digital age. Indeed, it is not a complete solution, nor is it an option for everyone.

Yet for those who can do it, a break from digital tech can help support new habits and screenfaring skills. A screen free week can provide a barrier between past habits and new ones.

After a hiatus from tech, there is an opportunity for a fresh start. It is easier to establish the kind of intentional-use habits described in these exercises. When I start from a baseline of no tech use, I can gradually add back only the digital activities I really want. This is easier than starting from a baseline of lots of tech use and trying to disentangle habits I don't like from everything else.

A tech fast can also be an opportunity to remember and discover activities, hobbies, and analog methods to accomplish things.

There is little that we can do about the historical conditions which led up to the present state of digital excess. Fortunately, much *can* be done to intentionally create barriers that contain some of the unhelpful psychological effects.

Tidy Computer Use: Avoid Attention Contamination

For the next week, make a point of following these three rules:

- Turn off your computer when you are done with it. Simply keeping it off creates a slight barrier, which will cause you to think twice before wasting time. It is not a major inconvenience to turn your computer on again, but it feels significant. (As side benefits, the machine will work better, last longer, and use less electricity.)
- Close any applications you are not actively using.
- Close any windows you are not actively using. It can help to keep bookmarks in organised folders. Instead of keeping every tab and window open because you 'might need it later,' bookmark them! That way they cease to be messy background distractions, but you can still find them later if necessary.

If you want help remembering, try placing something in your field of vision. A sticky note on your screen corner or an object placed in the fold between your laptop keyboard and screen can serve as a reminder: *close everything as soon as possible*. Similarly, you could wear a particular hat, ring, or bracelet for this purpose.

As a bonus rule, you can choose to keep your computer disconnected from the internet when using it for activities that do not involve internet connection. Only connect to the internet when specifically intending to use it—you'll save more power while creating another layer of awareness and deliberateness.

Cage Your Habits (or Put a Leash on Them)

Pick one of the following and integrate it into your life for the next week:

- Create a new login on your computer for focussed work. Keep it distraction-free, with only precisely the things you need for whatever kind of work you will use it for. Commit to never using it for entertainment, casual searches, or anything other than what it is dedicated to. Not even a little!
- Decide on specific hours of the day to which you will limit your use of digital technology. How many hours is up to you, depending on your needs. If you work online, perhaps the window is as broad as 8AM to 8PM. Or you could decide to only create a time window of one hour, say, only 4-5 PM. Whatever your window, stick to it *religiously*. Keep your computer and phone off the rest of the time (or, if you absolutely need to be able to receive calls, make sure your phone is free from non-emergency notifications). Do not be tempted to use them; if something comes up, write a note about it and deal with it during the next time-window.
- Choose a specific physical *place* from which you will access the internet (or two or three if necessary). For example, your home desk and your office desk. Limit your access to that place/set of places.
- Put your habits on a leash by connecting to the internet only via ethernet cable or some other form of physical cable that plugs in to your computer. Forsake wireless internet

connections. The visible connection will help create awareness. So will the need for a physical action to connect/disconnect.

Each of these strategies works to contain your digital-technology-related habits. Instead of them being ubiquitously present in every moment, they are limited to specific times, places, or digital places. You can *leave* the physical or digital places you associate with these habits and be free. The habits are in a cage, instead of you.

Pre-Set Intentions: Use the "One Thing at a Time" Rule

Try this once you are comfortable with using one of the digital habit cages above. The first time you use a computer each day, follow these steps:

1. Decide what you are going to do *before you turn on your computer*. Then stick to it!

2. If your intended activity involves multiple applications or sub-activities, reflect before starting: How you will know if you get distracted? What is the exact scope of what you are doing? A vague scope can allow one slight deviation from the activity to lead to another, and then another, without it being clear whether it counts as distraction or not. (Science teachers: this is similar to the idea of falsifiability. It can be a good way to practice the concept—the hypothesis "I am on task" needs to be falsifiable.)

3. If you catch yourself straying from your intended activity, try to recall how you got distracted. Walk yourself back step-by-step through each thing you clicked on. Do this from memory. This is extremely annoying, but that in itself will help deter you from future distractions. It will also teach you where your distraction-weaknesses are, so you catch yourself early on. What did you click on to get here? Before that? For example: *I was reading an article about space junk. What led me here? Before that I was reading about a new sci-fi show. Why did I start doing that? I was tempted to check my email, and I saw that my friend had started watching the show and highly recommended it. Before that, I was on task.*

4. Once you remember your way back to where the distraction started, proceed with your task where you left off.

5. If something comes up which makes you want to switch activities, close the computer, walk away from it, or otherwise distance yourself from what may or may not be a distraction. Think about whether it is worth changing your intention, and then return with a new intention if you decide to. Ideally, avoid this situation entirely—just do the new thing after you accomplish your original task.

6. When finished, start again at Step 1 if you have further tasks to accomplish.

7. Turn computer off.

To start with, only apply this to your first computer-based activity in the day. For example, maybe you need to check your email. Do you wish to respond to every email, just ones from certain people, or to not respond at all and just see what is in your inbox? Follow these steps, and when finished, distance yourself from your computer (close laptop, log out, restart computer, do something else—whatever works for you to create a clear before/after distinction). Then proceed with the day as usual.

When this is easy, apply it to the first and second things you do in the day, or for a set period of time (e.g., for the first two hours you are on a computer). Start small, and gradually apply this to more and more of your digital activity. It will greatly increase your awareness of distractions and your effectiveness to use digital devices to do what you intend to do, instead of what behaviour designers intend.

Kids can be encouraged to follow this procedure by allowing them greater autonomy in their device use if they demonstrate that they can be intentional.

A clear line cannot be drawn between manipulative and benign design. Behaviour designers will tell you they are making their products better, more engaging, more fun. This can be true, while at the same time those products may destroy lives, keep families apart, and result in minor harm such as regret over wasted time (adding up, across users, to millions of hours).

Fortunately, in spite of the title of this chapter, mind control does not actually exist—except insofar as we each have a degree of ability to control our own minds. You cannot truly 'control' another person's mind. Nor can an advertisement or a tech company. If you have control of someone's environment—which is relatively easy if it is a digital environment—you can shape what they value, and what choices they are aware of. You can train people to willingly (and not necessarily consciously) outsource their choices and behaviour to external cues. You can create associative links and behavioural habits which are very hard to get rid of. And you can *convince* people that they cannot control themselves or make their own choices—a belief which can become a self-fulfilling prophecy.

Even in their most aggressive forms, behaviour design and habit-forming technology are not "mind control" any more than, say, punishment or bribery. But their current level of invisibility makes them frighteningly powerful.

The next chapter will explore how those who create habit-forming technologies think about what they are doing. Learning about the techniques behaviour designers use to make their products 'sticky' or 'addictive' can dispel the invisibility. Having language for something makes it easier to perceive, identify, and respond to consciously. Fortunately, such language, and the conceptual understanding that comes with it, is not difficult to teach.

3. Rewards for Rats and Pigeons

"People joke all the time about trying to build a 'diaper product.' The idea is, 'Make something so addictive, they don't even want to get up to pee.'"

~Gabe Zichermann, expert on gamification and behavior design[16]

You have probably heard of the famous experiment of Ivan Pavlov involving dogs and bells. The Russian scientist would feed his dogs after ringing a bell. He found that after doing this repeatedly, he could ring the bell and the dogs would begin salivating—an involuntary response—even if he did *not* give them any food. He had discovered what is now known as 'classical conditioning:' an association (or linkage) can be formed between a sensory stimulus and an involuntary biological response.

In the 1930s, a man named B.F. Skinner was investigating the question of whether one could condition a *voluntary* response: could the type of stimulus-association Pavlov had discovered cause an organism to take a deliberate action?

To find an answer, Skinner and his team of graduate students kept pigeons in boxes. The pigeons were trained to understand that pecking a button would deliver them a food pellet; each box was equipped with an automatic food dispenser. A graphing device recorded the rate of button pecks. The pigeons, kept below a normal body weight by the experimenters, tended to press the button until they had eaten enough. Not a surprising behaviour in a hungry pigeon.

Like so many discoveries in the history of science, Skinner's key discovery was an accident. His lab was running out of food pellets, so he experimented with what happened when not every peck was 'reinforced' with a pellet. Instead of a reliable one peck, one pellet system, he set up his dispensers to only give pellets on some of the pecks.

Counterintuitively, this seemed to make the pigeons *more* motivated to peck the button. Intrigued, Skinner set out to test myriad variations. After years of experiments on pigeons (and a few rats), Skinner published a tome called "Schedules of Reinforcement," collecting his data on how different 'schedules' of delivering food pellets to animals affected the frequency with which they pushed a button.

Animals who were given 'reinforcement' after a set amount of time tended to slow down their pecking in between food pellets. If they had a visual indicator of how much time had passed, they stopped pecking until the time had elapsed. But if the food was dispensed on an *unpredictable* schedule—that was when they might peck, without pause, many times a second for hours and hours and hours. Even if less than 1% of the pecks were rewarded with a pellet. In fact, 'reinforcement' no longer made them pause to eat, or reach satiety—it encouraged them to peck *faster*.

Skinner believed that everything an organism does, including human beings, is a sort of mechanical result of past conditioning: outputs predetermined by inputs. To him, free will was an illusion. He saw his discovery of schedules of reinforcement as a hopeful one for society. If rewards could be used to shape behaviour, punishment was not so necessary. In his novel, *Walden II*, he envisioned a society which used behavioural training to create a utopia. Unfortunately for him, despite his good intentions he has gone down in history with his name attached to the animal experiment box he invented. He called it a conditioning chamber, but most people insist on referring to it as a 'Skinner box.'

> Would a society where people are motivated by rewards be more humane than a society motivated by punishments? The difference between rewards and punishment is not actually as clear cut as it initially seems. Take grades for example: is it a punishment or a reward to give a student a B+?
>
> It depends on the student, what they expect, and what they care about. If the student cares about grades, but only receives C grades, then a B+ is certainly a reward. For a straight-A student, it would be a punishment. For a student accustomed to only the highest marks even high marks are not a reward—they are merely the absence of punishment.
>
> What is experienced as a punishment or reward depends on the starting point. Receiving a reward over and over creates habituation to that reward; the absence of an expected reward is experienced as a punishment.

Skinner's strategy of unpredictable reinforcement, later known as **variable rewards** has been applied to many things. It became the basis for slot machines and the reckless, addictive behaviour they inspire in gamblers. Then, with the rise of the internet and digital technology, the same effect started to occur with things like email. People began checking it obsessively, far beyond what was practical. Like a pigeon pecking a button.

This, too, seems to have been an accident. Once the phenomenon was noticed, however, it began to be harnessed deliberately with greater and greater refinement. Silicon Valley developers who use behaviour science to create addictive platforms seem to be fond of referring to their creations as 'Skinner boxes:' the users, of course, being the rats or pigeons. Skinner's influence can be found anywhere from social media, to video games, to news websites, to many 'EdTech' programs.

Another scientist with confusingly similar initials enters the story here—B.J. Fogg. As a child, Fogg was fascinated by the idea of propaganda and the techniques used in advertising to persuade people.[17] He studied these techniques and soon began to see them everywhere. Later, apparently while reading Aristotle's *Rhetoric*, it occurred to him that one day computers, too, would be used to persuade people.[18]

Fogg went on to conduct experiments in what he called Computers As Persuasive Technology

('CAPTology'), and his ideas are foundational to an entire field of research. In fact, as far as I can tell he has coined most of the terms referring to the field: not just *captology*, but *persuasive technology*, and maybe even *behaviour design*. Fogg made a career out of teaching these persuasive techniques to tech companies and Stanford students (although he has since shifted focus towards helping people change their own behaviour).

Fogg's most influential theory is encapsulated in the Fogg Behaviour model, published in 2009. It depicts the elements necessary for a behaviour to take place: sufficient motivation, sufficient ability, and the presence of a prompt or trigger (in abbreviation form, B=MAP). The model's simplicity makes it easy to think about how to design an interface to encourage a behaviour:

"With great power comes great responsibility."
~Superman

The scientific method has allowed us to make immense gains in our understanding of the natural world. We can predict many things which could not be predicted before: if x, then y.

Prediction, to a large degree, allows for control: control of materials, giving rise to machines and sophisticated technologies, control of living beings, and, increasingly, control (or at least deliberate shaping and 'nudging') of human minds and societies.

Once the knowledge and ability to control something exists, the responsibility for this control cannot be avoided. Once you have a science of behaviour design, you cannot avoid behaviour design, because you still have to build buildings, institutions, and perhaps user interfaces, and you can approximately predict what effects these will have on their participants. What might responsible use of this knowledge look like?

you simply check if the three elements are present, and improve the design accordingly.

From the beginning, Fogg recognised the dangers of his model and the potential for abuse of persuasive techniques. In a 1998 paper on the possibilities of persuasive technology, he emphasized the importance of ethics in persuasion. Presumably recognising the likelihood that not all companies would try to maintain ethical standards, he also proposed a strategy to mitigate harms from unethical use:

> *"The best approach regarding the ethics of computers and persuasion is to educate widely about this new area of research and design… knowledge about persuasive computers helps people recognize when technologies are using tactics to persuade them."*[19]

It has been more than two decades now. Aside from a recent flurry of books, mostly aimed at professionals and managers, the education in question does not seem to have materialized. Let's see what we can do about that!

Meet Captain Hook: Nir Eyal's Hook Model

The Hook is one of the best-known models for how designers can build 'irresistible' habit-forming products. Nir Eyal came up with the concept while he was a student in B.J. Fogg's class. At the time, use of habit-forming techniques was already on the rise in tech companies, but information on the techniques was not widely available—it was concentrated in places like Fogg's Persuasive Technology Lab at Stanford.[20] Eyal says that he published the book *Hooked: How to Build Habit-Forming Products* to "democratize" the techniques already in widespread use among tech companies.[21]

Eyal's model is widely used because it distills a lot of the thinking underlying persuasive design in a memorable, practical format. This makes it a good way to get a handle on what the designers are doing. The Hook is divided into four stages: trigger, action, reward and investment.[22] They form a cycle, which strengthens a behaviour through repetition. I will summarise the model below, with additional comments highlighting impacts it can have that are not discussed in Eyal's book.

Trigger

A trigger is something that invites you to take a particular action. It can be an external stimulus, like an icon to click, an attention-grabbing headline, or a notification.

Triggers can also be internal: an external trigger, once ingrained in habit, becomes an internal trigger. Repeatedly clicking the Facebook notification icon, for example, can create an internal desire to check if you have notifications. This desire becomes independent of the icon itself—it can serve as a trigger without any need for an external stimulus. The mind provides its own trigger.

In Eyal's terms, there are also pre-existing internal triggers: states of emotional discomfort. Feelings such as loneliness, boredom, uncertainty, inadequacy, or anxiety can serve as internal triggers which encourage you to find a distraction, as you seek to escape from the unpleasant feeling. The Hook model recommends that companies find ways to channel these feelings into the act of using their product. Once ordinary emotional states become habitually linked to an action a company wants you to take, your own feelings become internal triggers which prompt you to use their product. All the major social media websites heavily make use of this strategy.

Unmentioned by Eyal in *Hooked* is that the negative feelings harnessed by companies might be increased by the very habits the model is used to create. Although some of the 'internal triggers' he discusses are an ordinary part of life, the *degree* to which they are currently experienced is not. The current high prevalence of feelings of loneliness, anxiety, inadequacy, and depression is at least partly related to the rampant abuse of habit-forming techniques.

Habitual use of Facebook, for example, can *create* feelings of inadequacy. Your feed might contain a stream of images and stories of people who appear, at least in posts, extremely successful and attractive. Your own life may seem to pale in comparison next to these polished, incomplete portrayals of others. It doesn't help that time spent scrolling timelines is generally time *not* spent pursuing your life goals. On top of that, constant exposure to rapid-fire bite-sized information can make it harder to focus when you do get around to trying to accomplish something. This, in turn, further reinforces a feeling of inadequacy. If that feeling is an internal trigger for more Facebook use, a feedback loop forms where negative feelings drive habitual use which drives negative feelings.

Other feelings such as loneliness or boredom can also be increased by similar feedback loops. Social media can enable human connections. But if the desire to connect with other people is hitched to aimless social media use, social media can take time away from nourishing social interactions, thus *increasing* loneliness. Alleviating boredom by watching extremely attention-grabbing, fast-paced videos can make the flashy gimmicks seem normal. This makes the world—the endlessly marvellous world—appear boring. Which might drive further video-watching, in the pursuit of something entertaining.

The same thing can happen for any desire one tries to fulfill online: I have often found myself endlessly reading or watching tutorials on how to make something for longer than it would have taken to make the thing I wanted to make. It felt easier than actually getting started. One or two sets of instructions is useful. It is less useful to use the false feeling of productivity from looking at instructions to replace the actual thing I meant to accomplish.

If an 'internal trigger' links with an action that genuinely helps with the problem or desire underlying it, you have the normal workings of motivation and action. It is quite a different story when an internal trigger is linked to an action that *appears* to be addressing the problem or desire, but is actually making it worse.

Harness uncomfortable feelings to profitable habits which cultivate more uncomfortable feelings (while discouraging self-awareness, reflection, and delayed gratification) and you get two things: the business model keeping much of the internet afloat, and the mental health crisis unfolding in heavily digitized societies. Many seven-year-olds have already learned to feel ashamed of their bodies and worry about looking 'sexy;' depression, anxiety, and loneliness are just the status quo.

FOMO, the Fear Of Missing Out, has reached epidemic proportions in the internet age. We are constantly being made aware of thousands of things we *could* be doing in any particular moment. We have 24/7 access to infinite media, whether news, movies, or conversations. It can be hard to choose, and maybe even harder to leave the screen to go do something offline. You might be missing out.

However, we've reached a point where it is obvious that we are *always* missing out, on basically everything. That is how it always has been, even if we weren't so aware of it before. FOMO is a bigger threat to the good things in life than the fact that we inevitably miss out on everything that happens in the world, beyond our own infinitesimally small corner of it. When I accept that this is the case, and that some missing out is the price of existence, FOMO loses its power over me.

Action

Drawing on B.J. Fogg, the Hook model emphasizes the importance of triggering extremely easy actions. One of the principles of the Fogg Behaviour Model (Behaviour = Motivation + Ability + Trigger) is that the amount of motivation which needs to be present for someone to take an action when they receive a trigger depends on how difficult the action is. The harder the action, the more motivation is necessary. In order to get as many people as possible to do an action, it is best to make it easy—that way, they do not need much motivation.

Another way to put it: to get someone to do what *you* want them to do, instead of what *they*

There is a grey area here around the meaning of 'control.' Those who create habit-forming technologies are quick to point out that they can't control anyone—they are just 'nudging' people, or making them more likely to do what they already want to do.

This is sort of true on an individual level, but is it true on a collective level? Companies record and analyse how different groups of people respond to different stimuli, allowing behaviour designers to tweak their designs to get more of the behaviour they are looking for.

If tweaking an interface makes 25% of people do something different than they otherwise would have, is it not reasonable to call that 'control'?

want to do, it helps when what you ask of them is only the tiniest possible thing—at least on the surface. A single click will do nicely. Rate this video. Follow this link. Read this message. Friend this person.

These tiny actions build habitual responses to digital stimuli. The actions are so easy that even *before* a habit is formed around it, the action might be only barely conscious or intentional (at least for those already experienced with using digital interfaces). Once an action is completely habitual, it can be hard for conscious intentions to get their foot in the door of the habit cycle again.

But for someone to take an action there still needs to be motivation of some kind, however small. How to motivate someone to respond to a trigger with a particular action? By shaping their expectations with carefully calibrated consequences.

Reward

B. F. Skinner's experiments on rats and pigeons showed that unpredictable (or variable) rewards are extremely motivating to these animals. Much research has gone into this phenomenon since then, and the effects are consistent across many animal species, humans included. Variable rewards have become a cornerstone of behaviour design.

If an action has a predictable reward, people (or animals) only take that action when they want to receive the reward. With repetition, this becomes boring; the action will only be repeated when the reward is wanted. A hungry animal will push a lever for a food pellet, but a satiated one will not.

However, rats, pigeons, and humans can get obsessed with an action if it results in unpredictable rewards. And, unlike the reward of food for a hungry animal—what psychologists call a **primary reward**—rewards in user interfaces are generally **secondary rewards** like social status, information, points, or currency. While there is a limit to how much food one can find rewarding, there is no limit to these secondary rewards. You never know what might happen, what benefit you might receive—so you keep doing the action. It's hard to resist because if you just do the thing *one more time*, maybe—just maybe—you'll hit the jackpot. It only takes a few seconds; what have you got to lose?

In *Hooked*, Eyal divides variable rewards into three types. "Rewards of the tribe" are social benefits such as status, approval, or new connections. "Rewards of the hunt" involve seeking and acquiring, whether material things, knowledge, or virtual 'treasure.' "Rewards of the self" involve task completion and increases in competence, such as 'levelling up,' or emptying your inbox.

Categories are handy for perceiving detail, but Eyal's system is not the only option. Rewards can be sorted in many other ways. Take any set of categories for human desires and apply it to the situation—you will find that all of them have been exploited by user interface designers in the tech industry in some form, unless it is physically impossible to do so (for example, websites do not currently emit pheromones). You can even make up your own categories: all you have to do is observe the strategies used and ask, *why is this being done? What desire is it fulfilling? What desire is it creating, or trying to create?*

The tragic thing is that the reason 'variable rewards' are so enticing to humans is that they help us learn and understand our surroundings. We evolved in an environment surrounded by complex beings that are difficult to predict—animals, plants, storms, other people. We developed a scientific instinct for curiosity and delight in discovery. We developed a desire to better ourselves, expand our knowledge and abilities, to excel.

Skinner points out in *Schedules of Reinforcement* (where the experiments which revealed the effects of variable rewards were first published) that it makes sense for an organism to ignore that which is predictable in its environment, such as food provided every time a lever is pressed.[23] And it makes sense for an organism to pay rapt attention to what is surprising or not understood in its environment: such things are the sources of danger and opportunity.

Attention to the unpredictable in a natural environment allows one to begin to unravel its mysteries. Complex beings like forests and friends cannot be fully understood, not even with all the modern technology you could hope for. But through sustained attention to the mysteries and surprises around us, we *can* gain practical understandings that allow us to roughly predict the results of our actions.

Apps that arbitrarily choose rewards to reinforce behaviors are not giving their users useful information. The instinct for curiosity and learning ends up hitched to an algorithm that spits out meaningless variation. What a tragic, tragic waste.

To be fair, not all variable rewards are arbitrary like this, and thus decoupled from meaningful learning. For one thing, rewards do not always need to be created by the designer, company, or

Supermarkets, with their shelves stocked with all kinds of colourfully-packaged, sugary treats, are a result of extreme control of a material environment, combined with the desire to sell edible products. Human beings evolved in environments where sugar was a rare treasure, so we have a bit of a weakness for it. We are not great at dealing with its abundance.

Similarly, we evolved in an environment which did not provide potent psychological rewards for tiny exertions of effort. I thought it would be clever to compare this with sugar, but it turns out behaviour designers beat me to it: "user interface candy" (UI candy for short) is a term used to describe design features, such as confetti in a congratulatory email, or cute bots which send unexpected heart-warming messages, which are supposed to create little moments of joy. Like sugar: sweet, and habit-forming.

algorithm. Eyal points out that, on social media and other platforms where people interact, *the users themselves can create variable rewards for each other.*

Many have compared social media apps, video games, and smartphones to gambling slot machines and drugs. They can be addictive for some of the same reasons.

But these new technologies have benefits that slot machines and drugs do not. They are multimedia, multifaceted, and while for one person they may be a destructive, even life-threatening addiction, for another they may be a life-saving source of information or community support.

Things change fast in the digital realm and there is a bewildering amount of diversity on top of that. Is it possible to separate the harms from the benefits in this wild frontier? Do governments have a responsibility to interfere? If so, at what point? Can they do so ethically?

This setup, which feels less artificial, can be subtly encouraged, facilitated, and guided by designers and algorithms. Variable rewards created by other people are not so arbitrary as algorithmic ones, although anonymous internet interactions can come close due to their lack of context (a lot of unrelated scraps of decontextualized information—such as a thousand YouTube video comments—are only barely more meaningful than random variation).

There are many cases where the 'rewards' are not decoupled from learning, such as the reward of finding useful information, or interactions with people you know (or get to know). These situations are less abusive of human curiosity, as they do not separate it from its purpose—though the platforms may still be selling personal data for profit.

Eyal and many others who write about persuasive design describe rewards as releasing dopamine in the brain. Dopamine makes you feel good, and tends to make you want more.

Investment

After receiving a reward, users are in an ideal state of mind for the final stage of the Hook cycle. This is the time to ask them for something more—an action that is not merely a click. People often do not anticipate that, by taking the simple initial action, they are being led to a more time-consuming one. Ideally, they do not notice this and simply go with the flow.

Being asked to do what Eyal calls a "bit of work" is effective because it encourages you to "store value" in a platform. Over time, you might put a lot of effort into building a profile, collecting contacts, photos, saved pages, followers, information, or notes in a particular website or application. (I would add that you may also store value simply by learning to use the interface).

Once all this content is stored and you have learned the ropes, it can be hard to leave. Learning another system requires more effort. There may be no way (or a limited way) to export the content you have painstakingly collected/created to some other platform, be it contacts or saved pages. Even if you want to stop using a platform—for example, due to concerns about data collection—you might just put up with it. An alternative platform with fewer drawbacks may be freely available, but to shift over might cause you to lose a lot of your 'investment.'

I would prefer to switch away from Gmail, for example, because I do not like the idea of Google collecting my data. But then I would have to tell everyone who might ever try to contact me about my new email address—a massive inconvenience. Besides, Google already has so many years of my emails and such a vast amount of data collected on me that it probably would make little difference. The switch has not happened yet. Maybe I'll do it next year.

On social platforms, individual 'investments' don't just store value for the people who make them, they provide value for other users. The users create the content—very convenient for the host company. Not only do your *own* investments provide you with reason to stick with a platform, other people's contributions do as well.

This can go even further than Eyal addresses. If a platform comes to dominate an area of life, the way Facebook dominates event organization in many communities, the investment of the collective into the platform can constrain the choices of individuals. Even if you are not on Facebook and do not want to use it, you can find yourself facing the choice to grit your teeth and make an account, or to be cut off from a large portion of the life of your community. Oh, so you want to find out when events are happening, but not have to scroll through Facebook while your personal data are collected? Too bad.

Another reason to ask users for an investment, not explicitly addressed in the Hook model, is that putting effort into something solidifies habits and strengthens commitment. The effort you exert reinforces the subconscious idea that the thing you put effort towards is important. You don't have to *think* it is important—your actions teach you to *feel* it is important on a visceral level.

This sense of importance, both at a conscious level (of stored value) and a subconscious level learned through exertion of effort helps strengthen the related triggers, completing the cycle of the Hook. Less and less external triggering is necessary, as the internal triggers, reinforced by rewards and investments, carry 'users' back to the platform again and again.

I have not included images of the Fogg Behavior model or the Hook Model here, to avoid the possibility of copyright infringement. For a visual representation, you can find them both online with a quick image search.

Naming the Problem, Revisited

The issue remains: how to talk about these techniques of 'persuasion' which are so deeply embedded in our lives, our institutions, and the current organization of the world?

There is no word that means "*to construct habits in people through interface design,*" or "*to have one's habits molded by interface design.*" Behaviour design is more of a field than a specific action. Habit-forming techniques are methods, not the act of applying them. Neither of these allows someone to conveniently label what is happening them: "*I'm so tired of Instagram trying to ____ me.*" Persuade? Coerce? Manipulate? These words can fit the sentence, but they are not very precise, and their accuracy is open to debate. We need something better.

I propose that we use a new verb: **impigeon.**

This word labels a problem that this book seeks to address, without getting into a tangle by also encompassing other things. To *impigeon* someone is to treat them like a pigeon in a Skinnerian conditioning chamber. It denotes an attempt to control a person's behaviour through an interface, and construct their habits through rewards and behavioural cues.

Pirates on the high seas sometimes take no quarter. Attention pirates, however, *always* take quarter, any quarter they can. They impigeon their victims—that's how they get their quarters. Amazingly, the quarters add up to billions and billions in ad revenue. Some booty!

This is not the same as actually controlling them. It does not imply successful control, but it does imply a shaping influence. There are also different degrees of impigeonment—it is not quite like imprisonment, where you are either in prison or not. I find myself a little bit impigeoned whenever I spend too much time on news sites or Facebook. Yet one can also avoid or escape impigeonment. I am only successfully impigeoned if I *allow* my behaviour to be designed by calibrated rewards.

The word does not take away our autonomy *or* give perpetrators of manipulative design a free pass. It carries an appropriate air of creeping unpleasantness. What person or company would want to be known as an *impigeonator*? Yet there are people who explicitly think of their users as Skinner box pigeons and design accordingly. This offense against the dignity of other human beings deserves a scathing label.

This word helps us get past other pitfalls of existing words. Behaviour design is an unavoidable part of interface design, and the word can include positive applications. The word impigeonment can be used to pass judgement on manipulative instances of behaviour design, labelling these as distinct. That way, such instances can be referred to without the linguistic acrobatics of a million qualifiers. Which makes important things easier to voice:

"Impigeoning people is not ethical."

"Your company keeps trying to impigeon people, and they are sick of it."

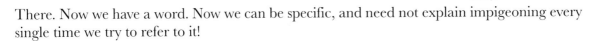

"I am teaching my children to be unimpigeonable."

There. Now we have a word. Now we can be specific, and need not explain impigeoning every single time we try to refer to it!

Exercises

For behaviour designers, models such as the Hook are useful for understanding the 'design space' for user interfaces. It helps them remember the available strategies, so they can exploit these more fully.

For our purposes, such models are useful for developing an eye for behaviour design. Just as a budding naturalist learns the shapes of different plant families and begins to see them more clearly, making finer and finer distinctions over time, such categories can help us—children and adults—become detectives of behaviour design. When we start to recognise and classify 'persuasive' design features, we start to interact with them consciously. When we interact with them consciously, there is far greater opportunity to choose how to respond, and to choose responses which align with our long-term interest.

"Mind Control" Scavenger Hunt

Using the framework of the Hook Model—trigger, action, reward, and investment—browse the websites and applications you use frequently to find three examples of each of these types of design features.

For each one, or at least one in each category, answer the following questions:

1. What does it make you *feel?*
2. What does it make you want to *do?*
3. What does it *mean* to you?

4. *What* does it look like? (colour, size, shape, symbolism, etc.)
5. *When* did you encounter it? (is it right after something else? what comes next?)
6. *Where* is it on the page/in the user interface?

7. *Why* does it look that way and appear at that time or place?
8. *How* might it be intended to affect someone?
9. *Who* might benefit from the result?

After this, write a reflection (or discuss):

- What patterns emerge in the answers to these questions?
- Did the design features you found fit neatly into the Hook categories of trigger, action, reward and investment? Were any hard to categorize?
- Which features were the hardest to notice and why?

In a classroom setting, these questions could be made into a worksheet. The scavenger hunt could also be open-ended: how many different Hook-type elements can the class collectively identify? Other possible approaches would be to have teams competing with each other to find as many examples as they can, or four groups looking at each of the different stages of the model.

Weird Wild Web Field Guide (or Bestiary)

Another way to develop a deeper understanding of habit-forming techniques along with the skill of recognizing them is to think about how to convey the information to others. Creating a field guide to common habit-forming techniques/design features which employ those techniques is one project that facilitates this.

For a playful and fantastic rather than scientific spin on this project, call it a 'bestiary.' The design features could become design creatures with their own persuasive powers, and represented as magical beasts or phenomena, for example the infinite scroll as a bottomless pit, or clickbait as a 'will o' the wisp' that leads you into the ad marsh.

Ideally, design features found during the scavenger hunt exercise can be used for this project. Alternatively, or for additional inspiration, you can find a list of common behaviour design features on page 121. For still more ideas, check out Chris Nodder's fifty-seven examples at Evil by Design: https://evilbydesign.info/

Step 1: choose a scope.

Just as a field guide tends to be for a specific bioregion, the scope of this project need not include the entire virtual realm. It could be limited to a single website, game, or social media platform. Or to a game genre, or social media generally. A narrowed scope may encourage more careful observation in finding design features and allow for a better grasp of the interplay between them. It also could allow kids to focus in on the corners of the digital world most familiar to them. These are the best places for them to learn to recognise how they are affected by persuasive design.

Step 2: organize the design features you wish to include.

Your goal is to create a field guide for people navigating a particular part of the digital world, which enables them to identify the different 'species' of habit-forming design features they encounter and learn a bit about each of these. What is the most useful way to organise it? By the action they encourage you to take? By website? By what desires they tap into? By a chronological sequence of when you encounter them?

Field guides for plants and animals are generally organized by how species are biologically related to each other or by where you tend to find them—but there are no standard categories for behaviour design features. Come up with your own classification and organization system based on what you think will be most convenient for people using your field guide. What works best will depend on the scope. In the realm the field guide addresses, what would make it easiest for people to look up what they find?

Step 3: create the individual entries for particular design features.

What information is most important to include about each? You may want to draw on characteristics you discovered in the "Mind Control" Scavenger Hunt. Pick a few you think are important to know and make sample pages for the field guide. Include a picture (or a few if necessary), perhaps with labels if appropriate. Choose how you will lay out different pieces of information. Where and when would you expect to find this feature? How does it work? What is its purpose? Is it dangerous? If so, how can you protect yourself from it? If you wish, you can make up some 'scientific names' that fit with your classification system.

Step 4: write an explanation how to use the field guide.

Be sure to include:

- If someone finds a feature they don't know the name of, how can they look it up in the field guide based on your organization system?

- Where to find different pieces of information in the entry for each feature/technique, such as the effects of a technique, it's usual 'habitat,' and self-defence strategies.

Step 5: have someone try it out.

The ultimate test of the field guide, of course, if for someone to use it. Find someone to test out your field guide (or sample pages) on. For kids, this could be parents or students in another class.

Screenfarer's Log: Fishing for Hooks

For a week, keep a daily tally of how many times you encounter habit-forming design features. Use a set of categories such as the four stages of the Hook model, or a set of categories made up for the Field Guide, or something else. You could also track them by time of day, or by what digital activity you are doing when you encounter them. Optionally you can track two different aspects at once, by creating a table: for example, columns could be stages of the Hook model, and rows could be different digital activities.

However, don't make it too complicated. The main point is the act of tallying itself. Try to catch every design feature that you see and note it in the tally.

At the end of the week, see if any interesting patterns emerge around which categories (or times of day or activities) have the most tally marks.

How Would You Design…?

An important angle to think through how behaviour design works is from the perspective of the designers themselves. The best way to do that is to do some designing.

Design your own video game, app, interactive website, or social media platform. The goal is to make it as fun as possible. Choose something you have experience with (don't design a video game if you have never played one) and start by thinking about the different designs you have encountered. What made them fun? Or not fun? You do not need to start from scratch—draw on your past experiences and put them together in a new, carefully thought-out way.

Plan out the following aspects:

- What is it for? What can it do?
- Who is it for? What will make it appealing to this group of people?
- Draw/sketch the user interface.
- Describe three aspects of the interface design. For each, explain:
  - What it does
  - Where/when it is located
  - What design choices you have made and why

After this, create a second design. Make it similar to the first and answer the same questions. This time, however, the goal is to 'maximise screen time' of people interacting with your design. In other words, make the design as *addictive* as possible. When you have completed this second design (with the aspects listed above), write a reflection on what you noticed:

- How are the two goals similar?
- How are the goals different?
- Are there different kinds of fun?
- What are the purposes of fun?
- Do you think it is easier to make a design fun, or addictive? Why?

With students who are keen on gaming, the following videos might be a good accompaniment to this activity. They are about humane game design, touching on the issue of fun vs manipulation from a gamer/game designer's perspective:

Progression Systems - How Good Games Avoid Skinner Boxes -
https://www.youtube.com/watch?v=S5camMoNw-o

Humane Design - Games Must Be Good to Their Players -
https://www.youtube.com/watch?v=GArkyxP8-n0

Hidden Game Mechanics: Design for the Human Psyche -
https://www.youtube.com/watch?v=sLXLlJ7FhJU

Understanding how the habit-forming technology industry models behaviour makes it easier to recognise their tricks in action, and respond to them deliberately. But models designed to help companies increase their user's unconscious behaviours have limitations when it comes to doing the opposite.

Like all models, they present a simplified understanding in order to tightly focus on their purpose. With the aim of cultivating a more intentional relationship with digital technology, we need to look beyond them.

The next two chapters focus on two important holes in the industry models. These two factors do not need to be taken into account when trying to encourage thoughtless behaviour, but they are key for *increasing* deliberateness and self-control. Bringing them into the picture can help us set up the habits we actually want to have, in today's impigeonator-infested digital landscape.

4. Meaning and Dopamine-ing: Does Everyone Really Like High Fives?

When an interviewer asks Ramsay Brown, co-founder of Boundless Mind, how his start-up helps companies get consumers addicted to products, Brown offers up his palm and asks: "Do you like high fives?"

After exchanging a high five, he continues: "Of course you like high fives. Everyone loves high fives. You love high fives because it releases dopamine inside your brain. It's the molecule responsible for what glues habits into place. If you can surprise or delight someone, in just little ways…you can activate this part of someone's brain to get them to come back and do the thing that earns them the high fives."[24]

Something key is missing from this picture. It's not just this one interview, either—the same logic is used in Nir Eyal's *Hooked*, by Tristan Harris of the Center for Humane Technology, and in every other explanation I have seen for how behaviour design works: giving people little 'hits' of dopamine keeps them coming back. Somehow, both those who create habit-forming technologies *and* those who seek to help people push back against those technologies seem to have completely overlooked what happens between the 'reward' and the dopamine: interpretation of a symbol.

Not everybody likes high fives. People who like high fives like high fives *because of the meaning they have learned to attach to them*. People in cultures where high fives do not exist might be confused, or offended, or threatened if you tried to give them a high five. It is not some kind of cross-cultural dopamine button!

> In Chapter 3, I defined *to impigeon* as *to treat people like pigeons in a Skinner box.*
>
> Another way to put this is: *to treat people as if they are dopamine buttons.*

There are rewards, such as food for a hungry person, which are not dependent on symbolic meanings. But pretty much all online rewards are based on things like status, money (or similar numerical abstractions), *pictures* of beautiful food, and so on. They can only be rewarding—or distracting—because of the linkages of habit and meaning associated with them. They are culturally dependant, symbolic, open to interpretation. Interpretations can be deliberately changed.

Take, for example, Facebook's 'like' button, one of the ways Facebook users can, in effect, give each other behaviour-reinforcing rewards. It consists of a little thumbs-up icon, with a number next to it showing how many times the icon has been clicked.

Silicon-Valley-types paint the reinforcing effects of the 'like' button as a result of pure, primal biology. But the number next to the button can only give someone a 'dopamine-jolt' *if* they have learned to interpret it as meaning something positive. One can transform its significance into something different, more complex, and less trigger-happy on the dopamine by digging a bit deeper.

Some elements of the meaning of the 'like' button are not open for interpretation. On the most literal level, the number of 'likes' is the number of people who clicked the 'like' button on a post. It would be possible to not know that this is what the number represents, or what a 'like' is, and such ignorance would make one immune to the 'dopamine jolt' that drives the habit formation cycle.

However, having learned this literal significance, you cannot simply choose to forget it. Besides, not knowing what online icons represent would be a great hindrance to anyone trying to use digital technology.

Fortunately, the literal sense of '*x* people clicked this button' is not the full extent of the like button's meaning, and it is not the reason for the dopamine. The other layer of meaning is *why* people clicked the button. Or rather, your assumptions about why they did.

The 'like' button's rewarding power comes largely from the idea that people clicked the 'like' button as a form of praise. On the surface, it appears to be a metric for how much the post, and by extension the person posting, is liked. By interpreting a number of 'likes' as approval from others, the person receiving 'likes' has a reason to feel pleasure from receiving 'likes,' rooted in the social nature of humans.

This interpretation seems straightforward and intuitive. But it is not actually very accurate. People can click a 'like' button for many reasons. Maybe they think you posted a gorgeous picture. Maybe they want to boost your confidence and be supportive, whether or not they actually like the picture. Maybe they want to be associated with your cause. Maybe they feel obliged to pretend to support the cause. Maybe they are worried that you will notice if they do not 'like' the picture, and it's easier to 'like' it than to worry about it. Maybe their friends 'liked' it. Maybe they want you to like *their* posts. There are many reasons to click the button, many reasons not to, and no way to actually tell what, precisely, 256 'likes' means in terms of human realities beyond simple clicks. The clicks are not particularly meaningful in and of themselves.

There is another *why* to the 'like' button: *why is it there in the first place?* The realization that Facebook is tracking your every move—collecting data on what you like and do not like to sell to advertisers so they can show you targeted ads—changes the meaning of the 'like' button. The realization that the like button is there to provide you with variable rewards that increase your habitual use of Facebook (so that you spend more time on it, can be shown more ads, create more content, provide more behavioural data, and generate more rewards for others users) further changes the meaning of the 'like' button.

Delving into the meaning of any behaviour-reinforcing digital reward in this way alters its effects. The more nuanced understanding of the 'like' button outlined above prevents the button from functioning as a straightforward punishment/reward mechanism (punishment if one receives fewer 'likes' than expected). Instead, the button becomes something more ambiguous. You may still choose to 'like' your friends' posts. Receiving 'likes' may still have an element of reward, but one that is easier to take emotional distance from. You have more choice in how it affects you.

For understanding habit-forming techniques, advertising is a fruitful source of comparison. It has been around for much longer than persuasive technology, yet the two have much in common and advertising is far more extensively studied.

Many ads rely on symbolism for their persuasive power, and that symbolism has been grotesquely overused over the course of the last half-century. This overuse is changing the meaning of the symbols used in ads, as people adapt to an ad-saturated world.

When I see an advertisement, say, happy people drinking a particular brand of soda, I don't look at it and subconsciously think: *wow, these people are so happy and attractive and have so many friends. I must buy this soda to be more like them!* (that is, the subconscious process the ad was intended to create). I look at it, fully aware of what ads are intended to do, and think *ugh, what an irritating attempt to control people. Does this stuff ever actually work?*

Having grown up in a world full of advertising, and been taught not to trust it, I am effectively immune to advertising gimmicks. Anything one perceives has some effect, and of course ads I perceive affect me in this sense. But they certainly do not make me more likely to buy things by instilling new desires (other than the desire to never see another ad). For me, the symbols leveraged by ads do not mean what the advertisers intend. There are no symbols that would, because I know what they are up to.

Behaviour design, advertising's mischievous offspring, can be defanged by cultivating this type of awareness. It may be more difficult, because the participatory nature of habit-forming technologies makes them more powerful, more 'sticky' than passive advertisements. Still, once you draw attention to the 'dopamine buttons,' once you change what they *mean*, they start to encourage thoughtful action instead of reflex.

Exercises

Symbol Dissection / Archaeology

This is an exercise in peeling back the layers of meaning that you associate with behaviour design gimmicks to see what is hidden inside.

- Find three examples of variable rewards (design features intended to 'surprise and delight') that you encounter on digital platforms.
- For each example, answer these questions:

o What does this make you feel?
o What does it mean on the surface?
o What else does it mean, intuitively?
o What desire is fulfilled by the intended meaning? What makes it a reward?
o What other possible meanings does the reward have?
o How does considering these questions change the associated feeling?

This type of questioning can be applied to any habit-forming features which cause you trouble in the future. As with the other awareness exercises, simply digging and paying attention to the details starts to change the habits themselves. Even the most careful archaeology cannot leave its artifacts untouched. For our purposes, that is a good thing!

Meaning Alteration: This Too Shall Pass

In a retelling of an old Persian story, the poet Edward Fitzgerald described a king who asked his minister to bring him a magic ring—one with the power to make a sad man happy, and a happy man sad. The king assumed that this could not be done. He was giving an impossible task on purpose. The minister returned with a ring bearing the inscription: *this, too, shall pass.*

Through the magic of words, the ring accomplished its goal. It could make a sad man happy and a happy man sad by redirecting attention, thus changing the meaning of any situation. You, too, can do this.

1. Find an example of a digital 'reward' that has an effect on you which you dislike (for example, by getting you excited and luring you away from what you are intending to do, or by making you feel disappointed because there was not enough of it).
2. Dissect what it means to you, in the vein of the 'like' button dissection above.
3. Consider what else it *could* mean. What is missing from the superficial meaning? Seek the nuance and complexity that you may not have noticed before.
4. Come up with a phrase that augments or alters what the reward usually means. It may draw your attention to other possible meanings, or the variety of them. For example, neutralizing the 'like' button with 'this number does not measure anything specific.'

From now on, when you encounter the 'reward' that you wish to alter the effect of, deploy your phrase and see what happens.

Tweaking what symbols mean to you on a small scale like this can be handy in the matter of dealing with habit-forming technology. But meaning can also be altered on a broader scale. This can provide a foundation for another part of human experience largely ignored by persuasive design: willpower.

5. Whatever Happened to Willpower?

This is a funny time to write about willpower. The scientific community studying willpower has still not fully regrouped after the widely accepted theories of Roy Baumeister began to have holes poked in them a few years back.[25]

Yet the subject cannot be avoided. Will is essential to every area of life, from academic achievement to social relationships. Intelligence and talent will not take a student anywhere without the willpower to direct and develop those gifts. No matter how smart you are, it is hard to get anywhere without the self-control to persevere through setbacks.

Habit-forming technologies make self-control all the more important. It is often the only barrier between one's intended use of time and clamouring hordes of digital distractions. Altering problematic habits formed by 'persuasive' techniques demands an effort of will. So does creating good habits—habits that help you accomplish what you actually want to accomplish. Habits can be formed unintentionally, without willpower getting involved, if they are created by behaviour designers. But it takes a period of conscious, willful effort to form a habit on purpose.

Neuroscientists are finally starting to confirm that self-control is decreased by certain digital platforms. A 2019 study found that playing World of Warcraft over the course of six weeks caused the

> We all have multiple motivations, and these can often be in conflict with each other. Cognitive psychologists think of this as a competition between possible behaviours, with the most compelling one winning.
>
> This creates an interesting situation when we consider the argument that behaviour design can't make anyone do something they do not want to do—it only can make it easier for people to do what they already want to do.
>
> This justification sounds decent until you consider the conflicting motivations. We all sometimes have desires to do things that would be terrible for ourselves or people around us. But the ability to restrain those desires is essential to having a society.
>
> Let's say I have an urge to break someone's nose (but *also* want to keep a level head and restrain myself). Is trying to nudge my behaviour towards violence okay, because you are simply helping me do what I wanted to do anyways?

parts of the orbitofrontal cortex in participants' brains to shrink. The brain region where the volume of grey matter decreased is associated with self-control.[26] Studies on gaming, social media use, internet addiction, and similar topics have been accumulating similar findings: brain regions responsible for self-control physically decrease in size, changing in ways that resemble the effects of chemical addictions.[27]

The research has not yet delved into the details of how these effects are tied to the design of the games themselves. It seems pretty likely that techniques like the ones in the Hook model have something to do with it, considering their widespread use and the fact that they are intended to reduce self-control.

We are creatures of habit, and this led B.F. Skinner to believe that free will is an illusion. Yet, the ability to will, to choose, allows us to create our habits deliberately.

How 'free' our will is or can be, in a philosophical sense, is an interesting question to debate. But it is beside the point: there is a very clear difference between acting in response to external carrots and sticks—especially immediate ones—and making choices based on some sort of internal compass, even if that compass is influenced by external magnetic fields.

Through will, we can choose how we construct ourselves. This certainly makes behaviour freer and less mechanical than it would be if it were merely inescapable habits created by external stimuli. Without the choice that will implies, freedom means nothing.

Willpower implies conscious decision, but in the models designers use to create digital platforms, conscious thought is mostly something to avoid. Drawing on the Fogg Behaviour Model, the Hook explicitly encourages training 'users' to take tiny actions thoughtlessly: the easier an action, the less motivation it requires, and the more likely a habit can be formed without even the effort of noticing it. 'Microhabits' and easy, thoughtless behaviours are emphasized in persuasive technology *because* they take conscious thought and will out of the picture. If too much thinking interfered, simple behavioural models would not produce such reliable results across large pools of individuals.

But what is this 'willpower' thing? There are various claims going around about willpower being fickle and useless. Or being 'debunked.' The kind of willpower that gets dismissed as fickle is often described as 'trying very hard to resist a temptation,' or 'forcing yourself to do something.' It is true that this does not seem very effective. A lot depends on how willpower is defined.

What I mean by **willpower** is *the ability to do what you consciously decide to do*. In other words, the ability to follow through on your intentions—including your intentions about what you will *not* do. This ability obviously exists. We have all experienced it. But how does it work? Why is it so hard sometimes?

Having played around with willpower exercises and found some success as well as some failure, I think there is an understanding of willpower that cuts through the confusion. Whatever generalized increase in willpower I have experienced comes from the increased value I place on willpower *itself*.

The ability to control oneself depends on how important one feels it is to do so, based on past experiences and imagined consequences. This is a consistent research finding which is not in question, and it makes perfect sense. If I believe that checking Facebook may cause me to lose 'just a few' minutes of my time, or better yet I believe it will be a good way to escape from doing my homework, it may be hard to stay on-task instead of checking Facebook. But let's say I believe firmly that checking Facebook when I meant to focus on my homework will result in sudden death: within seconds, my laptop will grow teeth and bite my head off. If I believed this, I would be *very* good at not checking Facebook. It would not even be an option. Clearly, higher perceived stakes result in better self-control.

When I put effort towards increasing my willpower, regardless of what form that effort takes, I start to feel that willpower is important in itself. The adage that "actions speak louder than words" does not just apply to situations involving other people: if you are trying to tell yourself that something is important, acting on it religiously is the best way to make the message sink in.

In addition to creating a feeling of importance through your actions, it doesn't hurt to also think of willpower as important. This is not hard when I realise that it enables everything I aspire to—if I do not follow through on my intentions, I will never achieve them. It is the key to living the life I want. All the emotional weight of my values and aspirations can lend gravity to the principle of willpower itself.

Once I start to value willpower in its own right, the value I place on willpower imbues seemingly small choices with importance—weighing in on the side of successful self-control. Not following through on my intentions is no longer a matter of wasting 'just one more' minute. It becomes a violation of the principle of willpower—by extension, a threat to my ability to live my dreams. Not *quite* as motivating as avoidance of sudden death, perhaps, but still powerful stuff.

This may sound melodramatic, but it is a crucial point: commitment to a general principle can consistently lend importance to smaller scale actions. Willpower, seen in this light, is certainly not the fickle thing some dismiss it as.

There are many ways each of us imbues small actions with great importance due to commitment to a larger principle. If you have ever worked overtime and lost sleep in order to do your job to the best of your ability, you were exerting self-control thanks to the importance you place on a principle. People who care about punctuality go out of their way to never be late. Parents routinely put their discomforts and temptations aside in favour of their commitment to their children and their parenting ideals. Followers of religions around the world do difficult things which are imbued with importance by their commitment to their faith—from fasting, to attending regular ceremonies, to taking vows of silence, and even enduring intense physical pain.[28]

Clearly, people *can* exert self-control consistently, with the right structure of

All this talk about willpower is not intended to imply that no one should ever have fun. Cultivating your willpower does not require all your actions to be planned and willful. Nor does it preclude ever acting on a whim or an intuition. Playfully acting on a whim can lead to wonderful experiences. Intuition can be very useful. And in a complex world we need to be able to adapt to unforeseen circumstances.

I simply mean to highlight the importance of having the *option* of self-control. Acting *only* according to whims is not freedom; it is enslavement to whims, and to any external influences that can generate them.

For playfulness and spontaneity to coexist with a strong ability to follow through on your intentions, you simply need to avoid acting on whims when they conflict with a past decision and avoid making decisions that inhibit spontaneity too much.

motivation. Commitments to deeply important principles, whether fairness or tradition, honesty or work ethic, enable self-control in situations where the principle is relevant (and one is aware that it is relevant). Many of these commitments will look like willpower in some situations, and not in others. Developing willpower across all situations can probably be most effectively achieved through placing high value on willpower itself.

Whatever you call it—willpower, self-control, self-discipline, accountability—once you have committed to such a principle, following through becomes easier. It stops seeming like a choice. Whatever you chose originally becomes the default course of action, and external interference cannot sway you so easily.

B.J. Fogg is one of the people who dismisses the role of willpower in forming habits. Instead, his advice to people who want to change their habits is to start small: create tiny habits, which require little motivation to get started, and then gradually increase them.[29]

Fogg's system seems effective. Changing habits with small steps is good advice. But combining both willpower *and* small steps is even better, particularly when our lives are so heavily shaped by habit-forming technologies. Incremental practice of willful action can build up one's willpower, and one's confidence in it. Unlike an individual behavioural habit, that incrementally built-up willpower is not limited to specific situations. It is useful in new situations, because by definition it applies across all situations that involve willpower. Thus, a strong will enables one to resist sudden unexpected temptations—the sort that habit-forming technologies target us with.

Willpower, as I have described it, is a meta-habit: a habit that makes it easier to form new habits, and to break old ones. What skill could be more useful than that?

Exercises

Screenfarer's Log: Willpower

For the following week, write a brief reflection before and after using your computer:

1. Before you use your computer, take a moment to assess your fatigue level and emotional state, and write a quick note to yourself on how well you expect you will stay on task. Are you feeling tired from the day and prone to distractions? Fresh and prepared to focus? Also include the date and time. Note any other factors that seem relevant, such as whether you are excited about your task or dreading it.
2. Use your computer.
3. When finished, look over your original note. How accurate was your prediction? Were you more distracted than you thought? More focussed? Make a second note on how things actually went compared to what you expected, and why you think this was the case.

Keep all of these notes together and in chronological order (on the same piece of paper, or in the same journal). At the end of the week, read over the notes, and reflect on the following questions:

- What did you learn from the process of reflecting before and after?
- What did you learn from reading over the notes in retrospect?
- When did you have good self-control? When not-so-good? Why?
- Do any patterns stand out? (expected or unexpected)

This exercise helps develop your awareness of how your willpower levels change throughout the day/week, and what conditions affect them. Excitement about your task can outweigh the allure of distraction. Tiredness makes it harder to have self-control. You can't hold as many things in your mind at once when tired—including thoughts which remind you of the importance to self-control. If you are aware of the conditions which affect your self-control, you can avoid putting yourself in situations which require a lot of it when you will have trouble managing them—such as navigating to a website that you know will show you enticing article titles, or watching a Netflix series which will autoplay itself.

Finding the Stakes

Create a journal entry answering the following questions:

- What are the most important things in your life?
- What do you most love to spend time on?
- What do you most need to spend time on?
- If you had perfect self-control, how would you divide up the time in your day?
- What are your long-term goals?

These are the things that are at stake in the matter of self-control. Whatever you want to achieve, whatever your ideal life, willpower is key to making it a reality. This could mean writing a novel, spending more time with your kids, running a marathon, or giving more to charity. It could mean finding more time to smell the flowers.

When you find yourself in a situation which demands exertion of willpower, call to mind your answers to the questions. Their importance will outweigh most temptations you will encounter. With practice, you will get better at remembering to do this at the right moments. Considering the stakes will start to help you consistently act the way you intended to.

General Willpower Training

Any small task or action which goes slightly against what you inherently desire can be used as willpower training. Deliberately creating an inconvenience, giving up something you like, putting up with a discomfort, resisting an urge, or doing a difficult task (including directing your attention in a challenging way) are all effective ways of doing this. These are all ways of telling yourself, subconsciously, that willpower matters: surely it must, or why would you have gone to all the trouble? Putting this sort of effort towards improving your willpower helps make it important on a deeper level than mere intellectual justification (though that is a good first step).

The *Focus Challenge* in Chapter 1 can be used repeatedly as a form of willpower training. So can the *One Thing at a Time Rule*. Many of the exercises in this book require you to direct your attention (increase your awareness of something) or resist temptations, and thus can be used as willpower exercises. You can also make up your own, based on the above paragraph. They do not have to have anything to do with digital technology to help you improve your self-control around digital technology; in fact, willpower exercises that are distanced from your existing habits may be the best way to start. Here are a few examples that I have used:

- Make your bed every day (especially if, like me, you don't care how your bed looks and are doing it entirely as a willpower exercise).
- Correct your posture. Whenever you find yourself slouching, straighten your spine.
- Carry around a non-perishable treat that you find tempting (such as a piece of candy or bar of chocolate) for a period of time—but do not indulge in it. At the end of the time, give it away.

We often divide motivations into short-term motivation or immediate gratification, and pursuit of long-term goals, with the latter taking more discipline. However, it is also technically possible to take actions which have no particular meaningful benefits or have benefits you do not care much about. You can use such actions for the purpose of training your will. The absence of other benefits ensures that the effort you put in contributes to your sense of importance for willpower itself, rather than the importance of the action or any benefits you receive from it. External rewards can deflate internal motivation, and this is the opposite effect: deliberately forsaking an external reward can strengthen the internal motivation of willpower.

Pick one of exercises above, or one that you have made up, and do it for the next week. Do not start doing multiple exercises at the same time; they work best one at a time, as small steps. If you get comfortable with one of them and decide to continue it, you can add another on top.

One of the reasons for the recent claims that willpower is useless or nonexistent is that, in some studies which were supposed to measure willpower, it turned out that people with high levels of 'willpower' had simply removed distractions and temptations from their surroundings (or just did not find them tempting in the first place). They did not exert self-control in the moment: they set up their life so that they would not have to.

Although this seems like more of a challenge to the experimental design (especially the willpower metric) than to the existence of willpower itself, avoiding the need to exert willpower in the first place can be a useful approach. This can be done alongside developing better self-control, for a two-pronged strategy. When it comes to removing digital distractions from your environment, there are already many apps and programs and plugins designed for this purpose. How to approach these is the subject of the next chapter.

6. Isn't There an App for That?

When I first encountered the idea of a smartphone app that helps you reduce your use of smartphone apps, I had to chuckle at the irony. But these days there is an abundance of such software. Many smartphones, laptops, and tablets even come with built-in tools to help you monitor, restrict, or reduce your phone usage, and a quick search will turn up hundreds of others.

So why bother with all these exercises?

Well, for one thing, the empirical basis for many of these apps is not necessarily solid. Most have not been tested to see whether they meet their goals. The design of such apps may be based on the intuitions of the creators, perhaps guided by one psychological theory or another.[30] This does not mean that they do not work—it means that it is up to you to observe whether or not they live up to their claims, and to notice any undesirable side-effects.

It is also likely that some of the apps which track you in order to help you use devices less (as some do, though not all) sell the personal data they collect to advertisers as part of their monetization strategy. Especially if the apps are free. After all, they exist in the same monetization paradigm as everything else. This does not necessarily mean advertisers will target you more effectively—maybe you have developed ad immunity and use effective blockers. Apps that track you may still be worth using, even if they sell your data, depending on your priorities—nonetheless, the tracking aspect is worth keeping in mind as a potential trade-off. It is even possible that the conflict of interest between a person who wants to reduce their device use, and an app seeking to collect data could motivate some app designers to intentionally *avoid* making their app as effective as possible.

Another reason not to rely exclusively on apps is that there are limits to what apps can actually do. While writing this book, I stayed offline most of the day, used a distraction-free computer account devoted exclusively to writing, set myself tight deadlines, and generally created helpful barriers to derailment, along the lines of those I have described in previous chapters. My attempts not to get sidetracked went very well—most of the time.

The things that *did* sidetrack me were things that an app could not have helped with. Sometimes, to avoid writing a daunting section, I found myself obsessively correcting minor formatting issues. Or, while conducting research, I found myself carried away by an intriguing thread of information that strayed further and further from the topic I meant to investigate—only to realize I had spent several hours reading about the Jevons Paradox or the social structure of medieval households instead of answering my research question.

An app that can distinguish between that and on-task research would be sophisticated enough to just do the research for you! And plenty of distractions are outside the realm that apps can influence. I also pulled a book off my shelf, which I have wanted to look at for a while. I thought I would just glance through—it might have relevant insights. It did. But the parts I read for the rest of the day were not so relevant. That may have been fine on a day when I did not have things to get done, but it became a hindrance to my work. No app could have stopped me from picking up the book and getting sucked in—only I could have.

Finally, the most important reason these skills and exercises are important is that one of the ways digital technologies can be harmful is by encouraging people to outsource foundational mental capacities to devices (see Part II for more on this). As a society, we are fond of finding high-tech solutions to all our problems. But the problem of being too reliant on technologies to do things for us cannot be solved by more of the same! Cultivating human abilities must be at least part of the solution.

With these pitfalls in mind, digital aids can be part of a viable strategy to create a more deliberate relationship with digital technology. Apps can help you:

Remove distractions from your digital activities. Sometimes it is necessary to visit websites laden with ads and flashy videos and clickbait, wading through a morass of 'external triggers.' Readerview modes on web browsers and plugins which block specific site elements (like ads or suggested videos) can reduce the number of distractions thrust in your face for you to willfully avoid. It is generally much easier to remove clickbait and ads than to constantly see them in your peripheral vision without getting distracted.

A limitation to this approach is that there is an arms race between advertisers and ad blockers—ads are increasingly integrated into what appears to be ordinary content, where they cannot be blocked.[31] Also, although web browsers and browser plugins have the authority to block specific features of how a web page presents itself, one mobile app typically cannot exert this level of control over another. The fine-grained blocking approach cannot be applied to all digital situations.[32]

Track your usage to encourage self-awareness and keep yourself accountable. When distracted, it is easy not to notice time passing. And it is hard to keep track of all of the distractions which happen (though doing this at least a little bit is a valuable and recommended exercise in awareness!). Apps which track your device usage for you can provide an objective measure of how good your discipline is and what you need to work on. This can even be a source of motivation. If you realize, for example, that you spend three hours a day scrolling through Instagram, the thought of what you could get done or enjoy with three more hours in the day could be a good reason to develop better self-control.

Disrupt very tenacious habits and make it easier for you to change them. Some applications interrupt you when you go on certain other applications. This brings an opportunity for conscious thought and decision into a process that has become automatic and unconscious. The catch is that it is possible to become habituated to the interruption. Have you ever left an object in your own way to remind you about a task you need to do, and then ignored it for weeks anyways? Apps can also lock you out of certain digital activities at certain times, or enforce limits on them. But these can be a way of outsourcing your self-control to an app. They may still be useful. Ideally, use apps which disrupt problematic habits as a transition stage, not an endpoint. If the app is working, you should only need it temporarily.

The key in using apps to combat unwanted digital habits is to use them to block what the Hook Model refers to as 'external triggers'—the various notifications, ads, and suggestions clamouring for your attention.[33] Avoid trying to use them to block 'internal triggers,' the internal feelings and desires that encourage you to seek out a distraction, or which lead you to a particular digital platform. 'Internal triggers' are better tackled with the exercises accompanying other chapters in Part I, or similar strategies. An example of the difference between blocking internal and external triggers:

Blocking an external trigger:

Approach: install a plugin which hides YouTube suggestions.

Result: distracting features are defanged.

Blocking an internal trigger:

Approach: lock yourself out of YouTube so you cannot go there to procrastinate.

Result: the desire to procrastinate may simply find another way to express itself; if you really want to procrastinate, you'll find a way with or without YouTube.

An application which, say, locks you out of Facebook is not as effective as learning to be disciplined about if and when you access Facebook and for how long. No app can prevent you from finding *something* to distract yourself—only your own internal barriers and habits can do that.

Habit-forming technologies cultivate impulsive action and weak willpower. Some of the apps which are supposed to help you mitigate its effects can replace the need to control yourself, remove the opportunity to practice self-control, and thus further contribute to undermining your willpower. They can simply become another form of dependence, acting as a sort of willpower prosthetic. Don't replace your willpower with a peg leg! Unlike a lost leg, willpower can be regrown. And there are a lot of things that willpower can do for you which peg-leg-willpower cannot.

Yet there is a place for digital aids to willpower. With an understanding of how self-control works, it is possible to assess what the effects of different strategies will be and choose ones that will work the best for you. A good starting place to assess apps and digital intervention for their helpfulness is to ask *What does this encourage me to practice?* and *What abilities is this replacing?*

What habits is this app creating? Are they freeing you from dependence, or simply making you dependent in different ways? How might they carry over to other areas of life? How might they backfire?

Exercises

Prune Away Online Distractions

There are many browser plugins out there for this purpose, often highly specialised. There are also instructions for changing settings in your computer or web browser to remove distractions. If you notice an annoying, distracting feature of a commonly used website, there is a good chance you can find a way to block it.

- Identify a place where you encounter derailing external 'triggers.'
- Find one plugin (or way of modifying settings on your browser) that removes the source of distraction.
- Install the plugin/change the settings and see the difference.

Once you have identified a distracting or annoying feature, the easiest way to do something about it is often to ask a search engine. I use a Firefox plugin to hide YouTube suggestions and ads, another to block ads in general, and another to remove the Facebook newsfeed. I found these with search terms like 'hide YouTube suggestions in Firefox' and 'block Facebook newsfeed.' The search engine method will also often turn up instructions for changing settings, or using features that your browser already has built in. Some browsers come equipped with adblockers, or with features like Firefox 'readerview' which strips away most of a webpage aside from the text.

Is This App Helpful, Harmful, or Useless?

Look up apps that are supposed to help you avoid distraction and combat compulsive phone or computer use. Pick one and investigate how it works:

- What are its goals?
- What strategies does it use to achieve its goals?
- Do the strategies align with the goals?
- What are users of the app practicing or not practicing?

Based on this, write an analysis which (roughly) answers questions like these:

- How useful do you think it is likely to be? Does it seem likely to achieve its goals?
- What might it be useful for, exactly? What specific problems might it help solve?
- Who might find it most useful? Is it a good fit for your needs?
- Does it create, reduce, or swap out dependence?

If you'd like a starting place for finding apps to investigate, one list of apps can be found here:

https://www.thelikemovie.com/resources-apps/

Having tackled the subjects of habit-forming technology, how it works, and counterstrategies (both mental and digital) to fight back against impigeonation, it's time to put all of these things together. Chapter 7 will show how the skills introduced in the exercises can be assembled into a complete toolkit for deliberate screenfaring.

7. Casting Off the Chain and Throwing a Reverse Hook

"It is every manufacturer's desire to drive its target customers to form a long-term habit of regularly using its product. Previous studies indicate that the habit of using a certain product can indeed be formed in a [systematic] manner, once the right sequence is followed."

~*Ang Liu and Tian Meng Li* [34]

Let's take a moment to go over the contents of Part I and fit them together, with the help of some visuals.

We have seen how habit-forming technologies work. They create a chain of mental pathways, which begins with something of emotional weight or practical importance. They encourage us to link these important things and ordinary feelings with use of a habit-forming product. Then this link is further enhanced through symbolic rewards, barriers to giving up use of the product, and a sense of investment. These reinforcements make the initial link between a feeling and using the product harder and harder to resist.

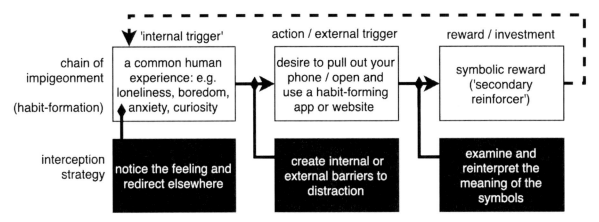

We have seen also how it is possible to interrupt this chain of associations in various ways. We can start by recognizing it and choosing not to play along—instead redirecting the initial practical or emotional need elsewhere. We can create barriers which interrupt the chain, in the form of physical inconveniences, digital interventions, and mental rules. In addition, through reinterpreting the symbols involved, we can change how the links of the chain connect and choose how we wish to be affected by 'rewards.'

But it is possible to go beyond understanding the chain of habit-formation and dismantling it. It is possible to create a contrary chain of association. In fact, this seems to be the structure of willpower (as well as other principles we can commit to). This contrary chain starts with something of great emotional weight, such as the ability to pursue one's dreams and find success in life. We can draw on this sense of importance to imbue a principle of willpower with importance. We can then use the importance of willpower in turn to lend importance to individual actions in which self-control is desired.

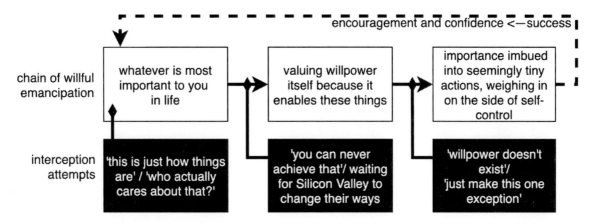

We can undermine the association-chain of habit-forming products. At the same time, we can create a contrary association-chain. One that increases self-control, and, by extension, freedom and choice. Equipped with these two complementary strategies, there is a lot we can do to push back against the negative aspects of the digital world, while still being able to take advantage of some of the resources and opportunities it provides.

When I compare the two chains, I find that they are not equal in power. The 'chain of impigeonment' is vulnerable to simple interceptions. The 'chain of willful emancipation,' once established, is extremely resilient. The black boxes in the second diagram show some ways that other people, one's own thoughts, cultural messages, and habit-forming technologies might interfere with the initial stages of developing a sense of willpower. But once the cycle is established, once you start to experience the benefits, these messages tend to fall flat.

Practice these two strategies, through the exercises presented in the previous chapters, or exercises that you come up with for yourself. The next time you encounter Captain Hook or other attention pirates, you will be prepared to deliver them a solid 'reverse hook:'

"Sorry, Captain Hook—but it was something I wanted to do anyways, and you were just too persuasive."

Habit-chains can trap us.

But they can also keep us safe.

And we can use them to go places
we could never go without them.

Habits can do so much for us—when we are in charge of them. Yet allowing behaviour designers impigeon us, allowing them to design our habits for their own gain, is not the only way habits can get us in trouble. The *absence* of essential habits can be just as much of a problem as developing habits that are distracting or harmful.

The next part of the book discusses how digital technologies can create such absences. One such absence has already been discussed in the willpower chapter. Other threatened mental abilities of great importance to all areas of life have their own chapters in Part II, along with exercises which help cultivate the missing habits.

In lieu of a formal exercise for the end of this chapter, I suggest going on a long walk or devoting time to something you love.

Part II: Skill–Replacing Technologies

8. Outsourcing Life Itself

Advances in technological sophistication often result in people **outsourcing** skills to the new technologies, whether on a personal or societal level. During the Industrial Revolution, many traditional crafts were outsourced to factories. Coopers, cobblers, and other skilled trades were replaced with production lines. This caused a decline in the particular skills associated with making barrels or shoes by hand. Outsourcing human abilities to specialists or technologies is nothing new, and it can open up possibilities for new skills to come into existence, like motorcycle riding and cinematography. But something more troubling is happening with digital technologies.

The potential for outsourcing is now incredibly comprehensive. It is not simply one skill here or there. Innovators are clamouring to create replacements for basically every human ability. I recently went to an end-of-year exhibit of projects from students at a design school. Among them were: an electronic device to 'help you connect with your kids,' a device to help doctors 'connect with patients' by letting the patient press one of four touch screen options to convey how they feel instead of using words, a 'smart' ankle brace that helps you notice if you are in danger of injuring yourself while dancing, a necklace that helps you notice your emotional state, an app that helps you figure out where to take a photo based on Google Maps locations where people had already taken photos, and (of course) a phone app that helps you use your phone less.[1]

Career preparation is an important role of education. Making sure kids build their digital skills at an early age can seem to be a crucial way to prepare them for the jobs of the future. This is often cited as a reason to give children access to digital devices early on. But the approach can backfire, because not all screen-time is equal. Many of the digital skills children are learning in their screen time are things like binge-watching videos, which will not exactly boost their future resumes.

In addition, these technologies are designed to be as easy as possible to use—and to do everything they possibly can for you. This can disrupt the development of abilities that are far more essential to success—no matter what the future looks like—than familiarity with current digital interfaces.

When everything is done for you, there is less opportunity to learn resourcefulness, critical thinking, or discipline. Constant exposure to fast-paced and attention-grabbing media can train children to be bored and expect the world to bend over backward to entertain them. This is the opposite of learning to be curious and seek deep understanding. No matter how important digital skills are as an asset in future careers, the cognitive abilities and character traits that excess use of devices can undermine are more important: creativity, memory, willpower, focus, curiosity, perseverance, empathy. And the digital skills that will be most important? Those that enable us to use digital technology without being used by it.

None of these designs enable new abilities. They take extremely basic abilities and replace them with a shoddy, less effective alternative, while encouraging atrophy of basic skills like *using words to communicate* or *coming up with your own idea for a photo*. Or, in a recent attempt to outsource kids' ability to make sound effects while playing with toys, the creative skill of *saying 'vroom, vroom' while pushing a toy car around*.[2] Not only is the replacement often a poor substitute—it can also take away the pleasure of doing the thing yourself.

In my teens I had pitiful social skills, little ability to navigate my own city without help from Google, a poor memory, a short attention span, and was not good at following through on what I said I would do. These issues were highly related to my use of digital devices, but they were not just the effects of habit-forming techniques and impigeonment—the effects of outsourcing were a bigger factor.

As they strive to appeal to the desire for convenience, commonly used digital platforms encourage us to outsource many abilities to them. It's not just willpower that can be replaced with a 'peg leg' in this manner. So can mental capacities that are foundations on which all other abilities depend. Memory. Imagination. Self-control. Attention control. Communication. Emotional regulation. Social skills. It is easy to allow devices to take the cognitive burden of these capacities off of your hands by doing them for us, or replacing the need for them.

It makes sense to use a prosthetic to replace a missing limb. We can't grow our limbs back. But it makes less sense to replace a *skill* with a prosthetic, just because it is weak from lack of exercise.

If Google lives in my pocket, I don't need to find answers to my own questions. Google will do it for me. I don't need to remember the answers, as I can always Google the question again. I don't need to speak to another person. My grandparents often tell me to google something instead of explaining it to me, but I would prefer to have the opportunity to hear what *they* have to say about it. Then the information would be more than mere information: a source of connection and relationship.

If I am using a digital product such as Instagram to escape from uncomfortable feelings (as Captain Hook would encourage), I am outsourcing my ability to deal with those feelings myself. I am becoming dependent on the product for emotional regulation. If I rely on point 'streaks' in a gamified educational app to encourage me to study, my motivation is outsourced to the app and becomes about the points, not about curiosity or learning. If I rely on hyper-engaging videos with fast-paced visual gimmicks to hold my focus on a topic, I am outsourcing control of my attention to whatever grabs it most effectively.

Using digital devices does not make us automatically lose all capacities. We have simply arranged our lives in such a way that it is often *easier* to rely on devices to do things for us than to do them ourselves. Humans, like many creatures, tend to take the easier option. When outsourcing our abilities is that option, atrophy is the result. In neuroscience terms, unused neural connections are 'pruned' over time. In everyday human experience terms, unpracticed skills get rusty. Digital technologies don't just create new habits—they also take some away.

Outsourcing and habit-formation interact with each other in complex ways. Outsourcing can enhance the effects of habit-formation. When willpower and self-awareness are eroded by outsourcing them to devices and external prompts, they can no longer serve as barriers to the formation of undesired habits.

In addition, when any skill is outsourced for long enough, it can seem like there is no other option but to use the device it was outsourced to. This creates dependence—other approaches may be forgotten, or at least come to feel impossibly difficult. For example, when I was in primary school, I knew my times tables. Recalling them was faster than using a calculator. Since then, I have drawn on this information so infrequently that, for certain multiplications, it takes a minute or two to check if I am remembering correctly. Because of this, a calculator is often faster. And the more I use a calculator to find the product of 7 x 8, instead of remembering it or doing the math in my head, the slower I become.

I don't really care if I can do math in my head quickly, which is why I don't practice it. What kinds of outsourcing are an issue depends, in part, on your priorities. I am very glad I did not grow up using autocorrect—then, I may never have developed an intuitive sense for correct spelling and grammar. Deliberately learning spelling and grammar rules as an adult would be a painful process and would make autocorrect look very appealing indeed.

Habit-formation can reinforce outsourcing, too. Habits become paths of least resistance: it is easier to follow an existing habit than to resist or break it. If you make a habit of outsourcing an ability, it becomes harder to stop outsourcing that ability the stronger the habit becomes.

Outsourcing is generally a *result* of following the path of least resistance. But sometimes, as with the calculator, outsourcing a skill to an app or other technological aid does not even save time or effort. At least, not at first. You might outsource because you are required to in school or at work. Or maybe you learned it from your parents, or peers. You build up the habit of using the outsourced method. Perhaps you just consider outsourcing 'the way it is done,' and have never learned another approach, or perhaps the skill of doing the thing yourself has atrophied. Once a habit is developed, it can *become* easier to follow the habit, even if, pre-habit, not outsourcing was easier. Even if the effort to stop outsourcing would save time and effort in the long run.

Because habit-formation and outsourcing can mutually reinforce each other, it is important to understand the two of them together. By not practicing mental skills, and allowing them to atrophy, we can become increasingly dependent on digital technologies as a crutch for the very weaknesses and deficiencies they create.

The most important ways to address outsourcing with kids are to:

Avoid giving them opportunities to outsource core mental abilities to technologies. Make sure they learn to write by hand, converse face to face, ask questions to real people, read books, and so on. Model this for them, too.

Get them outside and engage them in non-digital activities. Especially ones that are challenging, and exciting. And activities that help them develop the skill of recognizing the amazingness of the real, tangible world. Crafting, reading, sports and games like capture-the-flag. I emphasize outside, because daylight and distant views are essential for healthy eye development (a rare thing among the young these days), and because the natural world is full of never-ending interest and surprises, be it a wild forest or a back yard or a school garden. Not many kids will be glued to their devices when they *could* be climbing trees, making a campfire, or catching newts.

Part II of *Screenfarers* will not really address either of these. They are beyond the scope of this book, and have been written about by other people. I have included a Resource List (p.123) which contains some places to start, in case that is handy. But in the matter of getting kids outside, such resources are optional, not essential. If you take some kids to a forest or beach or creek and let them do their thing, you will see what I mean.

The following chapters provide some *supplementary* ideas. They contain exercises targeting specific mental skills which are suffering from technological outsourcing: attention, imagination, thought, memory, and human connection. These exercises and the accompanying information are for those who want to take screenfaring to the next level by helping young people bolster and value some of the mental capacities that are frequently outsourced to technologies.

Part II is also a celebration of the incredible things we can do *without* technological assistance, and an opportunity to get excited about these possibilities. A huge amount of the richness of human life and culture is neglected when we outsource as much of our inner lives as we currently do. Yet it is entirely possible to have access to both digital technology *and* that richness, if we make deliberate efforts to maintain and cultivate it.

Exercises

Analog Adventures

Identify things you usually use a digital device for. Pick a few and try doing them non-digitally. For example:

- Write a letter by hand to someone who will be happy to hear from you.
- Imagine a place you have never been, as vividly as you can, without looking up pictures.
- Try tuning an instrument by ear instead of using an electric tuner.
- Look up a word in a big, heavy dictionary.
- Wake up with the daylight instead of an alarm.
- Try using a slide rule instead of a calculator.
- Navigate by using a paper map, or by asking for directions.
- Find information in a library book instead of online.
- Learn a few of the clues that clouds, winds, bugs, and plants provide about oncoming weather and try to predict the weather from them yourself.
- Tell someone about an experience you had in detail instead of showing photographs.
- Sing a song instead of playing a recording.

Journal or reflect on what you learned from this. How did the analog experience compare to its digital equivalent? What was gained? What lost? Did trying a non-digital method for your activity change how you experience the digital approach?

Habits and Meta-Habits

Although I address attention, imagination/thought, memory, and empathy in separate chapters, these capacities are highly interrelated (Figure 1). Attention is an act of will—in cognitive terms, attention control is a part of executive function. Attention, imagination, and thought all play a role in the formation of memories. Memory provides material for thought and imagination, and is a source of identity, which is a basis for will. You will what you will because you are who you are—and you could not be who you are without memories of the past and the imagination to put them together into an identity-defining narrative.

Remember how everything is practice (or, at least, how it is useful to think about it this way)? *All of these abilities are, too.* Memory, the act of forming memories, is a habit shaped by what you consider important to pay attention to, and by the mental links you form between your perceptions and other things. An individual memory is also a habit: the habit of reconstructing a particular past experience in your imagination.

Similarly, willpower or self-control is the overarching habit responsible for the construction of individual behavioral habits. Your overarching ability to regulate emotions and empathise is responsible for the way your experiences translate into individual emotional patterns and habits of feeling. Figures 1 and 2 illustrate the difference between meta-habits and individual habits.

Individual habits formed by these meta-habits (Figure 2) can link up across habit types. Memories form connections not only with other memories, but also with other kinds of habits: emotional, behavioural, volitional, perceptual, cognitive.

It is important to think of the meta-habits as qualitative,

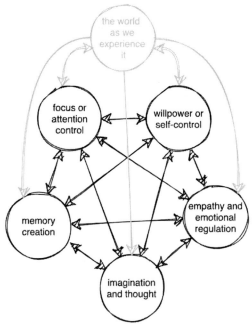

Figure 1. These meta-habits are the underlying abilities which enable the creation of the individual habits. They are interrelated and support each other.

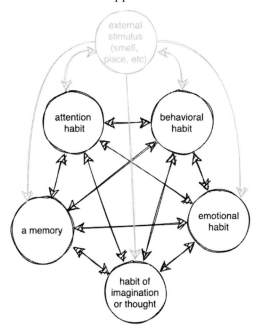

Figure 2. Individual memories, behaviours, imaginings, ways of paying attention, and emotional patterns can all link up with each other (and with the external world), forming chains and webs of association.

Can you imagine what would happen if one of the meta-habits in Figure 1 were missing? How might it affect the others? How might it affect individual habits?

rather than quantitative. One does not so much have an 'amount' of attention control, as a habitual style of attention control. For example, it is possible to cultivate the ability of paying attention to one's entire field of vision and having a very general awareness of one's surroundings; it is also possible to cultivate the ability to totally ignore one's environment in favour of reading a book.

One of these is not 'more attention' than another; it is different attention. Yet someone who is better at reading a book may seem to have poor attention when walking in the woods, and a child who is great at noticing everything around her may seem to have poor attention when sitting in a classroom.

From these building blocks and their interplay with the world around us, we construct our skills, our selves, and the world of our experience. Thinking about our mental abilities in this way allows for a more complex understanding of the habit-chains discussed in Part I. It becomes easier to see how such chains shape our inner web of associations. The approach presented in Figures 1 and 2 is also useful for tracing the effects of outsourcing across the interactions between different cognitive abilities.

As we consider different mental skills in the following chapters, it is worth keeping in mind how inextricable each one is from all the others.

9. Attention and Perception

Indigenous peoples around the world have perceptual skills which, to an outsider, can seem supernatural. Anthropologist Wade Davis portrays these abilities vividly. He describes how the Inuit can read reflections on the undersides of clouds like a map of the surrounding expanse of water, sea ice, and snow. How a Waorani hunter can smell animal urine forty paces away—and know what animal it came from. How the master navigators of Polynesia known as the Wayfinders can tell what island group lies beyond the horizon, by reading the pattern of refracted waves that is the unique fingerprint of each set of islands.[3]

Indigenous people worldwide also interpret the behaviour of birds to extend their perceptions of their surroundings. It is possible to know that a hawk is swooping from a particular direction without seeing it, that a bear is over the next ridge, or where an owl is sitting, silently watching for mice—just from the behaviour of nearby songbirds. This knowledge is not limited to Indigenous people, however: anyone willing to put in some time and attention can learn it. The examples I gave are ones I have personally experienced, and I am very much a beginner. I hear that the skill can get far more precise. A method for learning to understand the signals of birds has been codified in the book *What the Robin Knows* by Jon Young.[4]

> Immersion in digital existence in my early teens left me with the strange feeling that the internet was somehow more real than the real world. I walked around in the physical world with a sense of unreality, as if it was somehow all a movie set or dream.
>
> How far could such an inversion of reality go, for a child who learns to use an iPad before learning to walk? How might they grow up to perceive the world?

Animal tracking is another ancient skill which develops attention to detail and creative use of the senses (at the same time as deductive reasoning and imagination). Many skilled trackers, when looking at a set of tracks, find they can 'see' what the animal did. I once had the experience of looking at a set of tracks and 'feeling' what the animal did: in my mind, I suddenly felt myself trotting, four-legged, through a dog's footprints, recreating its motions.

Navigating, hunting, avoiding danger—these and many other human purposes come with their own modes of perception. Their own styles of paying attention, methods of noticing and sorting relevant details. From constructing buildings, to treating wounds, from climbing rockfaces to composing music, the ability to direct our attention opens up new worlds of possibility.

We have no excuse as a society for raising children who think the world is boring if it isn't talking to them at 400 words per minute while flashing bright colours. We can do better.

"While we tend to describe the internet in terms of distraction, what's being developed, when you check email or Facebook neurotically, or get sucked into Candy Crush, is actually a particular kind of focus, one that prioritises digital motion and reward."

~*Micheal Schulson* [5]

Attention is our window to the present, letting in the experiences that become memories from which we construct the past and imagine the future. There are different kinds of attention, and we get very good at the ones we constantly practice. That includes the form of flitting attention the internet tends to cultivate, which we often refer to as 'distraction.'

Attention *control* is a subcategory of willpower: the ability to pay attention to what you decided to. Distraction happens when other things appeal to you more strongly than your commitment to your intention. The less committed you are to your intended object of attention, the easier it is to be distracted.

Not all of the distractingness of the internet is by design. A lot of it is simply absence of barriers combined with ordinary mental habits.

Anyone who has tried some form of meditation can attest that an untrained mind will wander hither and thither, zipping down random-seeming mental rabbit holes without needing any assistance from the internet. It is extremely hard to get a grip on this flow of mental chatter and direct it intentionally, which is what various forms of meditation aim to do. It takes patience, discipline, and practice.

The way we typically browse the internet is analogous to these mental rabbit holes. A meditator has only the contents of his or her own mind as sources of rabbit holes. But when we use the internet, the entire world wide web is eager to help us distract ourselves. For this reason, intentional screenfaring may be even harder than meditation, though the two have much in common.

Some things we perceive with our senses are inherently more attention-grabbing than others. Online content is often designed to grab as much as possible. Bright colours and movement contribute to this; so do loud sounds, and catchy melodies.

But an identical sensory perception is not necessarily equally engaging to different people. That which you have practiced paying attention to can much more easily snatch it away from something else; that which you have practiced ignoring cannot as easily be a distraction. I find it hard to read outside, because I have practiced paying attention to birds and plants and winds. When I am outside, I can't *not* pay attention to them.

Habits of attention can be altered by changing external stimuli, or by changing one's responses to them. I could go inside to read, without the birds distracting me. I could also persevere, pointedly ignoring the birds, until ignoring them becomes a habit. This takes more effort, will, discipline, but means that with practice I will be able to read outside— but I also may notice less about my surroundings.

Exercises

If you pay attention to your attention, you can improve your habits and strategies, through self-knowledge and noting what works. You have already been doing this by following the exercises in Part I. Many of them involve attention control and directing attention towards self-awareness. Here are a few more ideas to play with, in the realm of attention and perception.

Question Challenge: Awakening Curiosity

When we are curious, it is easy to pay attention. Lack of curiosity can stem from not having paid enough attention to something to discover what is fascinating about it, or from not seeing the connections to other things which make it significant. There is no lack of detail and mystery in the world—but if we don't even realise that the mystery is there, it is hard to be curious.

Pick a topic or object. Now ask a non-stop stream of questions about it for five minutes. The questions can build on each other but do not say anything that is not a question. See how far you can go and how creative you can get. How varied can the questions be about a single thing?

In a classroom, this could be done in groups. It may help to provide a few example questions to get the questions flowing.

Scientific discoveries are not made because the scientist had precise math skills or collected data meticulously. Those things may contribute, but the real source of discovery is the ability to notice what others miss and ask a truly original question. Why do objects fall to the ground instead of floating away or levitating in the air? Where did the diversity of lifeforms come from? Does gravity affect light itself? Much of the rest is just procedure.

We risk stripping the mystery out of the world when we think we know things that we don't. Current attitudes towards science can create the impression that more or less everything is already scientifically understood. Cataloged, classified, *finito*. No need to pay attention for yourself. The frontiers of knowledge can feel like they are distant and fast receding.

The reality is that there is a lot we encounter daily which is not understood by scientists (who are more aware of this than the rest of the us). And even for things which are understood, personally discovering or rediscovering them makes for meaningful and memorable learning.

Science is powerful, but there is no reason for it to remove the wonder and mystery from life. Approached the right way, it instead allows us to encounter new sources of awe and mystery which were previously inaccessible.

Exploring the Senses

In modern culture, we tend to rely on our senses of sight and sound more heavily than any of the others. And even these, we do not necessarily develop to their full capacity—so much of what we are looking at or listening to is designed to be obvious and easy to perceive at a glance, be it traffic signals or infomercials.

If we slow down and take the time to play with our other senses, we can discover a lot we are otherwise missing out on.

A good way to start is to close your eyes and see what you can perceive about your surroundings. This can be especially effective outside, where much is happening that you may not be aware of. See if you can find five new sounds/scents/textures you've never encountered before. Ask questions about what each of your senses can pick up. Focus on one at a time, and try to stretch it as far as possible. After delving deeply into each sense separately, see if you can combine multiple senses while still picking up as much detail as before.

Here are some ideas for questions and activities which contribute to this process:

Touch
- *Is the air moving? What can your skin tell you about the shape of air currents around you?*
- *What temperature is it? Are there multiple temperatures in different places? How humid is it?*
- *What can your feet tell you about the ground? Is it smooth? Carpeted? Rocky? Springy?*

Try moving through a physical space based on touch. You could start with your own home, and then try an outdoor space like a forest. Or, say, an obstacle course built from gym equipment. With a group, one person can provide a navigational reference in the form of a sound (clapping, instrument, voice) and other people can try to follow the sound using their sense of touch.

Try doing a familiar activity blindfolded, such as drawing, washing dishes, playing an instrument, or knitting.

Find a large plant (or tree trunk, or a complex 3D object such as a carving) and try to build a picture of it in your mind through touch alone. What shape are the leaves? How are they arranged? How does it branch? What else can you learn through touch? As a partner exercise, this can be done like 'meet a tree,' where one partner leads their blindfolded companion to tree (or plant), lets them explore it through touch, and leads them away again. The challenge is for the blindfolded partner to find the tree or plant again afterwards.

Pass around a series of unusual objects and try to notice as much as possible about them by touch alone. It can become a game to figure out what they are.

Smell
- *How many different smells can you distinguish in the air?*
- *What direction are scents you pick up coming from? Are there different smells at different heights?*
- *Do familiar objects that you use regularly have a smell? Can you recognise them by scent if someone else holds them up for you?*
- *Can you find anything that does not have a smell?*

Create a treasure hunt based on a scent trail, using a fragrant substance such as an essential oil to mark out a route to something that is hidden.

Taste
- *Does the air have a taste?*
- *What ingredients can you detect in your food? Can you detect all of them?*

Try eating lunch with a blindfold on. Does food taste the same when you cannot see it? Try eating with a clothespin on your nose. Then take it off and see the difference.

Sound

- *What is the quietest thing you can hear? Can you hear anything inside your own body?*
- *Can you hear anything on the ground around you?*
- *What can you hear to the west? Can you hear upwards?*
- *What are the lowest and highest sounds you can hear?*
- *Can you hear any sounds that you do not know the origins of?*

Go outside in heavy rain and close your eyes. See if you can build up a 3D image of your surroundings based on the sound of raindrops hitting different surfaces, at different heights. (Trees, buildings, varied vegetation, etc are helpful to have nearby for this purpose).

Sit in one place and try to map all the sounds you hear for 15 minutes. Come up with a visual notation for different kinds of sounds and use it on your map. What direction are they coming from? How far away? What do they sound like? When did they happen? How can you represent these?

Sight

Try making full use of your peripheral vision. Gaze straight ahead, but without focussing on anything. Without moving your eyes, notice different parts of your field of vision. It can help to stretch your arms out sideways and wiggle your fingers—how far back can you move your hands before you can't see your fingers wiggling anymore? If something moves in your field of vision, try following it with your attention but not your eyes. Try following multiple things, such as flies or snowflakes or cars or shivering leaves.

Observing a Place

Find a place that you can visit at different times of day. (It need not be far away—it could simply be your back yard or the street you live on). Over the course of a week, spend time sitting in this place and observing as many different things as you can. What kinds of animals and birds can you see? What about insects and spiders and worms? How many different living things can you find? What is each of them doing? If there are people, who are they, when are they around, and what are they up to? If it rains, what paths does the runoff follow? What would the place look like if you were the size of a mouse? What would it look like if you were the size of an ant? Does the place smell different at different times of day? Where exactly is the sun rising and setting? If possible, try to visit at odd hours of night as well as different times of day. See what you can discover. At midnight or 3 AM there might be things happening that would happen at no other time.

Record your observations in words and drawings. Take notes, write poems, create sketches and maps—for example, maps of the different sounds and smells from different times of day. You could extend this by writing a story from the perspective of something you saw (such as a squirrel, a house, a raindrop, or a fire hydrant).

10. Imagination and Thought

"Once men turned their thinking over to machines in the hope that this would set them free. But it only permitted other men with machines to enslave them."

~Frank Herbert, *Dune (novel)*

Philosopher David Abram describes imagination as "the way the senses … have of throwing themselves beyond what is immediately given, in order to make tentative contact with the other sides of things that we do not sense directly." [6]

Imagination allows us to take limited information and extrapolate beyond it, whether it comes from the senses, or is communicated through language. This is also true of thought, which cannot be meaningfully distinguished from imagination. Examining the stuff that makes up thought, one finds that its substance *is* imagination. My inner monologue consists of imagined sounds, but I can also think in imagined spatial relationships, mathematical symbols, and tactile sensations. For other people, the experience is different. Some do not 'hear' their inner monologue, but instead 'see' written words, or find that their speech muscles twitch in ways that correspond with particular words. Some people think more in pictures.

The rational kind of thought often prioritized in education is built upon this foundation: reason is simply the application of certain rules to the raw imaginative material of thought. Only computers can use logic without imagination—but it would be a stretch to call this thinking.

Imagination organizes and extends our knowledge and perception. I know what is on the shelves behind me right now in my imagination, though they are not in my field of vision. I can imagine the consequences of doing something dangerous without having to experience them. When faced with a choice, I can perceive the future trajectories of my options. These perceptions are guesswork, of course, but nonetheless they guide my choices. I can be considerate of others to the extent that I can imagine and predict their feelings from subtle outer signs.

Without imagination, not only is there no art—there is also no science. It takes imagination to pose new questions, crystallize data into new theories, apply logical reasoning, and design experiments. There would also be no empathy, no literacy, no language, no abstraction, no planning. We can perceive the future only through imagination—without it, as far as our experience is concerned, there would literally be no future.

But in a flood of information, how can one practice the skill of 'throwing' the mind beyond what is available? If the content never ends, where is there space for imagination?

The inventor Nikola Tesla probably contributed more than anyone to the creation of the electronic technologies we take for granted today. He had around 300 patents to his name, including patents that were essential for the development of radio communication, X-rays, the current design of electric motors, electric turbines, neon lights... he even created the alternating current system for transmitting electricity, which enables modern power grids.

Tesla had an extraordinary imagination. He didn't draw his inventions—he constructed them in his mind. He could vividly 'see' all their precisely measured parts, assemble them, and set them moving. He claims that if there was a measurement error or imbalance in his design, he would see it in the imagined construction and correct it before building the invention in reality.

Some of this may have been a gift of genetics: as a child he formed extremely vivid memories and would see a detailed picture of an object flash in his mind's eye simply from hearing its name. But he also trained his imagination: sometimes the visions he had disturbed him, so he practiced picturing other things until he could journey through entire worlds in his mind. Worlds which felt as real as the one he experienced with his senses. Tesla credits his accomplishments not to his innate skill, but to this training. He also credits his powerful will, his ability to do whatever he set out to do, which he also deliberately trained.[7]

Imagination is not something that just happens. Imagination, creativity, and thought emerge out of an alchemical blend of challenges that require them, varied experiences, curiosity, attention, and long hours of daydreaming. They require practice, which most reliably occurs when it fills a need of some sort—whether deflecting strange visions, staving off boredom, or solving pressing dilemmas. Never exercising one's imagination is a sure way to have a weak one. Fortunately, imagination practice can be great fun.

Exercises

Imaginary Senses

Close your eyes and imagine an edible object that you know well, for example an apple. Look at it in your mind's eye and try to see it in as much detail as possible. Notice the colours, textures, blemishes, and so on. Rotate it around and 'look' at it from all angles.

Now 'touch' the apple in your imagination. Can you 'feel' its surface? How much does it give if you squeeze it? How does the stem feel? What temperature is it?

Now imagine holding the apple up to your ear and tapping on it. Can you hear it? Take a bite. Can you hear the crunch? Can you taste it? Feel it in your mouth? Take an imaginary knife and slice it in half. Can you feel the knife move through? Hear it? Smell the fragrance from the slice?

Whatever object you choose, try to interact with it in your imagination in a way that covers all the basic senses. Notice:

- Which senses were the hardest to imagine?
- Were there any you could not imagine at all?
- Which senses were most lifelike and vivid?
- How vivid were they in comparison with real-life perceptions?

Although not everyone can develop a photographic memory, everyone *can* improve on their imaginative abilities. These do not all come in the same form; different people imagine in different ways (often with different senses), though the reasons for this are not well understood.

I, for example, had no visual imagination but an extremely vivid imagination for sounds and tactile sensations—until I trained myself to have a very vague visual imagination by trying to picture things over and over in different ways till I slowly improved. There seem to be benefits and disadvantages to both imaginal senses of this sort *and* the lack of them; it is not necessarily 'better' to be able to imagine with every sense. It is also possible to learn to imagine in new ways, through practice, which suggests that this too is at least partly a matter of habit.

Exploring what your imagination can do both strengthens it and teaches you your strengths. If you know what forms of representation your imagination relies on, it can be easier to remember things effectively, because you can structure memories around, say, words and sounds, or pictures, or whatever you find most vivid. What you imagine most easily is also typically what you pay the most attention to. What you practice imagining can shape what you pay attention to and remember.

Bringing Words to Life

In many fantasy stories, characters have the power to make words become real, solid things, whether through magic spells or other devices. We can do this, in our minds. The more we do it, the more 'real' our imaginings can seem. Stories automatically get us to engage our imaginations to some degree. However, this can be enhanced by doing it deliberately.

Try reading or listening to a story, while deliberately enhancing the imaginative process. Whatever is being described, strive to experience is as fully as possible with all your senses. It may be easiest to start with listening (say, to an audiobook) instead of reading, because that way you can close your eyes.

If doing this exercise with children, this is a great opportunity to read out loud, taking it slowly and perhaps inserting reminders, if those are not already present in the written text (*What does the fur feel like? What does the wind sound like?*).

Once you are imagining the story as richly as possible, start asking questions, as in the "Question Challenge" in the previous chapter. *Why did this thing or that thing happen? Why was this detail mentioned?*

Engaging your imagination in these ways makes the story you are reading more memorable. Even if you struggle to, say, picture things (as I do) the act of *trying* still strengthens the memories you form.

But this skill applies far beyond stories. Good stories are already written to engage the senses and facilitate imagination, which makes them helpful training material. With practice, the skill of bringing words to life can be extended beyond stories to anything else: lectures, textbooks, dry academic papers, philosophical arguments, and data spreadsheets. Forms of reading or listening which many people find boring and unmemorable can become vivid, interesting, and memorable if you master the skill of throwing your mind beyond the words.

A word of warning: if children practice this too much, they might start to find everything fascinating—every school subject, and many things besides. This can be overwhelming. And peers who think it is 'cool' to be bored may not understand.

The No-Googling Challenge

How often do you type something into a search bar without thinking about it? Heck, I recently did this so thoughtlessly that I didn't realise the search bar was actually a messaging box, and I messaged one of my professors my search terms instead of searching for them!

Search engines are the mass teleportation devices of the information world. They instantly teleport millions of sources of information to you at your whim. This can be extremely useful for finding things, but it can be overused. The point of this exercise is to make search engine use more deliberate, while highlighting other options (as well as the hidden costs of search engine overuse). What you choose to use search engines for after the challenge is up to you.

1. For the next week, whenever you have an urge to Google something (or use any other search engine), pause. Ask yourself:
   - Is the question of practical importance, seeking information you need to act on? If so, consider whether the practical need can be fulfilled in another way, say, by asking someone. If you must, you can make an exception for finding information you need immediately.
   - Is the question simply something you are curious about? If so, instead of googling, go on to step 2.
2. Explore the question with your mind (if you do not have time to do this when the question arises, write it down and explore later).
   - Search your memories: what do you already know that relates to your question?
   - Identify what is missing: what pieces of information would you need in order to answer it? What possible factors could affect the answer to the question?
   - Consider how you could fill the gaps: Can you figure out any of this through observation? Can you extrapolate any of it from things you already know?
   - Guess and imagine: make up some possible answers. They do not have to be correct. Make the guesses as detailed as possible.
3. Periodically (each day or week) look over your list of things you felt an urge to search.
   - Has thinking about them led you to thoughts you may not have otherwise had?

- How many of them are still interesting to you? How many seem like a waste of time?
- Did you answer any of your own questions? Are some still bugging you?
4. When the challenge is over, search for one of the questions you explored with your mind. Reflect/journal/discuss:
    - How did the results of the search compare to your guesses?
    - How did the analysis process alter your intake of the information you found?
5. Notice what you remember, or do not remember from this experience.

An alternative version of this, if you find that you have to use search engines for work, is to only restrict non-work-related searches. Another is to set aside a single hour (or less) of the day for searching, and otherwise follow the directions outside of that hour.

11. Memory

Give a child a mnemonic, and she might remember a fact. But *teach* a child how to create mnemonics, and she'll remember whatever she wants for the rest of her life.

Throughout most of the recorded history of Western civilization, memory was considered an art, and the Art of Memory was considered an essential part of education. The earliest records of it are from Classical Greece. Ancient orators used places to help them remember the sequence of topics in a speech. They prepared for the speech by placing memorable objects and characters along a route through an imaginary place. While performing it, they 'walked' through their route to 'see' these imaginary reminders. This and similar techniques were called the 'method of loci' but are now often referred to as a *memory palace* or *mind palace*.

The Art of Memory was practiced as a routine part of intellectual life for well over a thousand years, evolving over time. In the Middle Ages memory was upheld as a virtue and was applied more to religious matters instead of political and rhetorical ones. Many scholars believe that the some of the wackiness of Medieval art was a result of intentional use of the Art of Memory principle that *strange things are more memorable*. In the Renaissance, the Art was taken up and further transformed by real-life magicians such as Giordiano Bruno. Many early scientists practiced it, too. Sir Francis Bacon apparently had a room in his house designed for use as a memory palace.[8]

Memory traditions are certainly not limited to recorded European history. Oral cultures around the world have their own versions of the art of memory. For the Australian Aborigines, the physical landscape they navigated is overlaid with a web of stories,

People have used places to help them remember for millennia. More recently, we have discovered that the hippocampus, a part of the brain essential to memory formation, is particularly good at dealing with spatial relationships.

Digital technologies often make spatial relationships fluid and thus useless to memory. Text on a website typically rearranges itself instead of staying in a fixed position—unlike text in a book, which is in a certain chapter, on a certain page, and has a spatial location on that page (have you ever found something in a book by remembering what part of the page you saw it on?).

Search engines take this to another level, by teleporting you results from all over the world, without spatial ties to each other and other things. These free-floating search results are not just hard to remember because they are easy to look up again—they *also* have lost all spatial qualities that make it easier to store them in your mental treasure chest.

The Ancient Greek practice of associating places with topics is where we get our word *topic*. It comes from the Greek word for 'place,' *topos*. Remnants of the word's original meaning still exist in words like *topical* and *topographic*.

called *songlines*, which were associated with different features of the land. In this way they store both their culture and practical information about plants and animals which is essential for survival.[9] An old anthropological study on the Navaho found that they classified—in memory—over 700 species of insects, most of which were not of practical day-to-day importance; the knowledge was pursued and remembered for its own sake.[10] When the Matsés, a people in what is now Peru and Brazil, recorded their orally transmitted medicinal knowledge in book form, it filled a 500-page encyclopedia.[11] As extraordinary as this sounds, memory techniques are so widespread in cultures around the world that the memory techniques of the Greeks may well have been inherited from earlier oral cultures.[12]

If anything, the absence of them as a central part of a culture is more unusual. The art of memory is still an evolving tradition today, though it has become a relatively niche pursuit. Still, bits and pieces of old memory systems are scattered throughout our culture. Scraps of the art of memory have found their way into modern pedagogy in the form of mnemonics and learning theory. And the stories mapped onto the stars in Ancient Greece still inform how we name and divide the constellations today: Cygnus, the swan; Pegasus, the winged horse; Orion, the hunter, son of Poseidon.

We know that there is a relationship between digital technology and the erosion of memory. Everyone who engages with the digital world has experienced this first-hand, within themselves. Educators encounter evidence daily in their students. One of the consistent findings in the scientific literature on how digital tech affects the mind is the link with decline in memory.[13]

But, of course, 'digital technology' is not a single uniform experience! What, exactly, is the connection between digital experience and memory?

It is easy to remember something when:

- You have **grappled** with it (given it thought, attention, effort).
- It is **remarkable** (strange, surprising, striking, evocative).
- It feels **important**.
- It has order and follows **patterns**.

These four principles are my own paraphrase from a set of principles followed in the Middle Ages.[14] They also match up with a set of principles I derived from examining my own experience of memory, prior to reading about the Art of Memory.

I may have chosen the order of the principles presented here for mnemonic purposes, but I will leave it to you to puzzle out what the mnemonic is.

Digital technologies interact with all four of these principles. Although digital interactions *could* be designed to support memory, this is rare. Most digital platforms aim for convenience instead. A bit more detail on each of the principles can help reveal some of the mechanisms by which current digital tech habits are eroding memory:

You have **grappled** *with it (given it thought, attention, effort).*

Thinking about something involves making links with what you already know. Some of these links may be random associations with other contents of your mind. Thought may also result in understanding, which inherently works as a mnemonic—the best kind—by fitting new information into a model or existing body of knowledge.

Even if you cannot reach understanding without more information, thinking about it still helps in two ways. One, you create a place for missing pieces to fit into, strengthening the surrounding knowledge and linkages. Two, putting effort into the attempt tells your mind on a visceral level that it is an important subject—when you do come across answers, or arrive at understanding, you won't be inclined to forget.

This is subverted by easy answers right away, and lack of time to dwell or revisit.

It is **remarkable** *(strange, surprising, striking, evocative).*

If something one needs to remember is already remarkable, so much the better. This principle can also help us remember even the dullest things by creating associative links between what we need to remember and things that are striking, amusing, strange, or otherwise emotionally engaging.

The internet provides access to such an overload of these things that their strangeness can be dulled. This can reduce the relative weirdness of things we wish to remember. We are habituated to a lot of strange things these days, so we get a lot of practice forgetting them.

It feels **important.**

You are viscerally motivated to remember something if you deeply care about it—or if you know there will be negative consequences to forgetting (especially if you have *experienced* this). Situations can be deliberately created where there will be meaningful consequences to forgetting, to internalise motivation to remember.

The importance of remembering something is subverted by the idea that 'I can just look it up.' This idea gives you an excuse to practice forgetting.

It has order and follows **patterns.**

Recognition and understanding of patterns that already exist can aid memory: they fit into a model or existing knowledge base. Verse forms with metre and rhyme make poetry more memorable for this reason. If there are no inherent patterns to use, patterns and order can be artificially imposed, for example representing information as a mnemonic acronym, or as a series of images linked by a story.

Information which is removed from context is harder to remember because the context often provides the order and pattern which aid remembering. Much online information is presented without much context, and one can also move through many contexts online too rapidly for them to provide structure for memory formations.

Remembering grants us abilities that the external memory of 'I can just look it up again' does not. A well-stocked memory is essential for tasks such as synthesizing ideas, discovering patterns in information and experience, creating new knowledge. It is the basis of thinking for oneself, and for judging what to believe or disbelieve. Too much reliance on external memory can leave one dependant on the ideas and interpretations of others. Memory also has a synergistic relationship with understanding: a thing that is understood tends to be remembered, and a thing that is remembered is more likely to be understood.

> The four principles above seem to apply not only to memory but to other kinds of habits—habits of behaviour, thought, attention, emotion. Can you see how?

We need not memorize everything, of course. Some things *are* more important to memorise than other things. All information that we take in through our senses is filtered by our attention, and then further narrowed down as it is stored in memory—this is an important part of how we make sense of what would otherwise be the overwhelming chaos of the world. There are many things I prefer to write down instead of bothering to remember them.

Yet memory's importance extends beyond utility. It is integral to meaning-making and identity formation. When you commit something to memory, it becomes a part of you, maybe forever. You have a relationship with the material. This is why I run poetry events in complete darkness—one of the effects is that it forces people to memorize the poems they present. Hearing a poem read aloud is not the same as hearing a poem recited by heart. There is something particularly intimate, touching, and beautiful about a recited poem. A poem memorized becomes part of the way you perceive the world and yourself. So, too, does anything stored in memory. Memory systems from around the world involve an interplay between the practical need to remember useful information and the art of filling one's mind—one's inner world—with that which is most beautiful and meaningful.

Exercises: Memory

Memorising the Unmemorable

A good way to understand how mnemonics work in general is to take one of the hardest things to memorise—random arbitrary numbers—and apply a simple mnemonic. Most people find it very hard to remember more than 7 numbers in a row. But it is possible to remember far more than this, very rapidly, if you have a way to *make* them memorable. I have been amazed at how effective the following method is. Everyone I have taught this method to succeeded at remembering the entire string of digits.

1. Write down a random 13-20 – digit number.
2. Set a timer for 3 minutes.
3. Make up a mnemonic to remember this sequence of digits:
    a. Look at the first digit and think of an image which has a similar shape—for example, a 2 looks like a swan neck.
    b. Look at the second digit and come up with an image.
    c. Now imagine the two of them interacting in a bizarre way.
    d. Come up with an image for the third digit.
    e. Link the third digit-image to the second by making them interact.
    f. Continue until you have memorized the whole number, or the timer runs out.
4. Hide the number.
5. Write down the number from memory.
6. Reflect:
    a. How many digits were you able to remember? Did you get them all?
    b. If you forgot any, why did you forget? What did you do differently from the other numbers?
    c. Did anything other than your image sequence help you remember the number? (For example, doubled digits, or a few digits that happened to be similar to your phone number).

An alternate approach is to use rhyming words instead of shapes. This technique can be further systematized and sped up by creating a set of images for the digits 0-9. Or, with more effort it can be possible to store more digits in the memory in longer sequences by coming up with images for 00-99.

This can be used to memorise historical dates, phone numbers, and so on. More importantly, with a little tweaking the basic technique can be applied to any kind of information; pretty much anything is easier to remember than random numbers! And, just like how reading practice can allow sounds and meanings to leap off the page into your mind as fast or faster than you can say them, memory techniques can be practiced to the point where you can construct mnemonics for whatever you want to remember, as you are reading it, hearing it, or experiencing it.

It might sound incredibly boring to memorize random numbers, or the order of a deck of cards. For people who compete at such tasks in memory championships, however, it is actually extremely entertaining: the only way to memorise such boring information is to *make* it extremely entertaining. The memorisers transform the meaningless numbers into vivid, dramatic, hilarious images and stories. However, memory is not exactly a spectator sport.

What Do You Forget? Filling Gaps in Natural Memory

Memory theorists distinguish between natural and artificial memory, but by the latter they are not referring to a smartphone. The distinction has been around since classical times. **Artificial**

memory is what you used in the previous exercise: creating arbitrarily made-up associations to encode information in a memorable form. **Natural memory**, if applied to the previous exercise, would be simply relying on your ability to remember the numbers without such associations. For other kinds of information, it also consists of remembering things based on the conceptual links inherent to them: for example, remembering the meaning of a word by learning its etymology and how to use it in a sentence, or remembering the that red light has the longest wavelength of visible light by its position in the spectrum and its proximity to infrared. (As opposed to remembering a word's meaning based on a pun, or remembering that red has the longest wavelength by picturing a long-haired surfer, covered in bright red sunburns, riding a huge wave). There is a lot of grey area between natural and artificial memory, but the distinction between the two is still useful.

Natural memory can encode more useful information, without adding in relatively arbitrary associations. Artificial memory can be very helpful in situations where natural memory fails us. Through understanding how associative linkages work in both natural and artificial memory, we can extend our natural aptitudes into areas that we struggle with. For example, I play music and find it easy to remember melodies and song lyrics—but I forget what songs I know. To help myself remember, I organise song titles into acronyms and geometric shapes.

1. Write down things you find easy to remember on one half of a piece of paper and things you find hard to remember on the other. Try to recall varied situations where your memory failed you, or pleasantly surprised you.
2. What patterns emerge? What particular kinds of things would it be useful for you to remember better?
3. Identify one of these key areas (e.g., names, the guitar chords for songs, phone numbers) and design a simple mnemonic system to fill the gap.
   a. What do you need to remember?
   b. What *part* of this thing do you need to remember, to have the rest of it spring to mind? (e.g., the first line of a song).
   c. How can you represent these pieces of information vividly and memorably? (e.g., the letter A becomes a famous person whose name starts with A wearing an avocado costume and holding an armadillo; a reminder to buy flour becomes a giant loaf of bread with flowers growing out of it, etc.)
   d. What organized set of things that you *already* remember can you use as a memory aid? (e.g., the letters of the alphabet, landmarks on your walk home, the arrangement of furniture in your house, the number images you made in the previous exercise, a song, poem, story, or set of characters you know very well).
   e. How can you vividly and memorably link the things you need to remember with the set of things you already remember? (e.g., an alphabet of people/characters each interacting with one of your vivid reminders; imagine a bizarre scene for each item to remember taking place at each landmark on your familiar walk; connect reminders to each event in a story).
4. Practice the system you have come up with. Tweak it if necessary.
5. Try applying your memory technique to the memory task you previously struggled with.

12. Connection, Empathy, and Learning from People

"We used to live in a world in which there wasn't enough information. Information was currency. Now we're in a world in which there's too much information. There's information absolutely everywhere... Google can bring you back a hundred thousand answers. A librarian can bring you back the right one."

~Neil Gaiman [15]

I struggled with whether I should write this chapter at all. Thanks to my years of self-observation while disconnected from the digital world, I had a pretty good idea of what was going on with the mental capacities described in the previous chapters. I found that understanding supported by the scientific literature. But I can't say I understand what the digital world has done to my emotional life and ability to connect with other people. I don't know what can or cannot be traced to that source, I have little basis to imagine what the absence of digital influence would look like, and I'm not sure I have any good advice about what can be done in this realm. I certainly have not unravelled the issue for myself. Even if I had, I'm not sure I would want to discuss it here. It is more comfortable to focus on mental abilities that are more practical and less personal.

Nonetheless, this facet is so important I cannot leave it out. Although I cannot comprehensively address how empathy, human connection, and emotions are impacted by particular uses of digital technologies, there is an aspect of this which I can speak to.

Empathy involves imagination, a form of imagination most easily exercised through interactions with real, flesh-and-blood people. Some of it comes built-in, in the form of the mirror-neurons that register the emotional expression of other people, animals, or even cartoon characters and cause a similar feeling in oneself. But empathy is also a skill, which develops through attention to others, care for their feelings and experiences, and the ability to imagine their inner world based on one's own experiences.

At its best, the internet has the potential to stretch our empathy. We can find ourselves relating to people whose shoes we would never have had the chance to imagine ourselves into before. But all too often, it can do the opposite of this. It can remove relationship from our interactions, hiding human beings behind text on a screen. It can allow us to imagine others as if they are flat cardboard cut-out characters, not people with real lives, cares, and complexity. Perhaps it is this tendency that lies at the heart of the alarms being raised right now about political polarization. But this tendency does not just create societal conflict. It can flatten our emotional lives and all our relationships if we are not careful.

Forming bonds with other people is something we are generally inclined to do by nature, but it does not just happen on its own. It requires interactions, shared experiences, affection, mutual attention. And throughout human history (and prehistory) a huge part of what created these shared experiences was the need to teach each other things, whether sharing knowledge between peers or handing it down to the next generation. When this ancient, basic task is mostly replaced by digital technologies, what happens to the fabric of our relationships?

I have been teaching naturalist skills, such as plant identification, for about four years. As a result, friends often turn to me when they want to figure out what a plant or bird they encounter is called. Recently, while I was walking with one such friend, someone we met raved to us about a smartphone app which uses machine-learning to identify plants for you. I could see my friend becoming interested—the app would make it easier to figure out what all these plants are. And I could see myself being replaced, made obsolete by an app.

It is easier to discover what a plant is called if an app does it for you, certainly. It means you do not need to develop an eye for botany, learning to recognise the markers of different plant families in order to narrow down the options. Nor do you need to remember the name you learned (you can look it up again). Nor do you need someone on hand to provide guidance.

But when someone asks me the name of a plant, I do not just tell them the answer like an app might, so they can forget it right away. Based on my knowledge of the person, I encourage them to stretch their memory. I tell them to look closer, to see what they can notice and figure out themselves. Maybe after that I will give an answer—if I think it will be beneficial—or maybe not. They will not only remember better, they will remember more: the smell, the rough edges around the leaves, the muddy area the plant likes to grow in, the tiny hairs on the stem.

Perhaps more important than the effectiveness of different methods of learning is that the knowledge I treasure most is knowledge I have learned from people. The captain of the first ship I sailed on taught me constellations while we were on a night watch together, pointing them out with his green star-laser that seemed to touch the sky. These are not just more memorable but more *meaningful* than constellations I learned from the internet. As a musician, my tech-free experiment meant I had to learn songs from people. When I play those songs, I feel like distant friends are at my side, even though I may never see them again.

Having learned so much of what I know from the internet, these meaningful scraps of knowledge-learned-from-a-person are relatively few. For a person from a pre-digital generation, knowledge would be much more often linked to human relationships. I have read books where characters mentally 'hear' the voice of a parent or mentor repeating a characteristic piece of advice, but have very seldom experienced this. Most of the information that shapes me came to me as just that—information—not as advice from a person.

I have been deeply grateful for the times when someone has had the patience to personally teach me something. I delight in the opportunity to do the same for others, sharing the too-rare experience of learning from fellow humans. Other, more 'efficient' sources of information can *seem* to make this sort of relationship obsolete. But only if we fail to consider the relationship itself, as if all that matters is information and the convenience of its delivery.

Learning does not happen in a vacuum. *How* one learns plays a large role in *what* one learns. It is not the same thing to learn something from an iPad and to learn something from one's grandparents, friends, or teachers. Learning from other people situates knowledge in a web of connections and pre-existing relationships, not to mention that it also forges those relationships in the first place.

Learning from the web, paradoxically, can have the effect of *not* situating what is learned in a web of context and meaning—it allows for learning decontextualized trivia, which one arrives at by random chance in a storm of other out-of-context content. Not everything on the internet is like this, of course, some of it is scaffolded and highly contextualized and designed for educational purposes, and some interactions happen between people with meaningful relationships—nonetheless, the internet creates more potential for information without meaning than perhaps any other medium.

Exercises

Connected Learning

Learn something from a person. Ask someone to teach you something, call up your mother for a recipe, learn a new family story, ask for advice or directions. Whether a friend, family member, colleague, stranger, or student, whether older or younger, learning from someone gives them the opportunity to shape your life. People with skills or knowledge are often very happy to share what they know with others. In the age of infinite online tutorials, they may not get many opportunities to do so! Although there are times when it is inappropriate to ask someone to teach something, and people are sometimes too busy, in many cases it is an honor to be asked.

Once you have learned something from one person, expand on that. Try to learn something from:

- A family member
- A friend
- A stranger
- Someone much older
- Someone much younger

How is what you learned coloured by who you learned it from, how, and where?

Empathy Stretches

One way to exercise one's empathy (and ability to imagine context for something where the context may not be obvious) is to read a viewpoint that is very unfamiliar or perhaps contrary to your perspective and try to understand where the author is coming from.

1. Think of three groups of people whose views you find strange, mysterious, or unrelatable.
2. Pick one group and write a journal entry describing what you find strange, mysterious, or unrelatable about this perspective.
3. Write down at least five questions about the perspective.
4. Find several short pieces of writing from highly intelligent, eloquent people within this group.
5. Suspend criticism! Read these pieces with the intention of understanding where the author and target audience are coming from. What do they care about and why?
6. Assume, while reading, that you do not necessarily know what they mean by what they say, why they are choosing the words they are, or what their motives are. At the same time, try to imagine your way into these things. The point is not to dismantle, disagree, *or* agree. Simply try to understand.
7. As an extra step, imagine how other topics would look from this unfamiliar perspective, or to imagine how someone within that perspective would view your own attitudes.
8. Write a reflection on what surprised you, how your understanding of the perspective you examined has changed, and anything else you learned.

I try to do this, or something like it, whenever I start to be overconfident in my own views, or when I catch myself dismissing a perspective out of hand based on a very simplified understanding.

If everyone engaged in this sort of exercise regularly, we probably would not have insane levels of political polarization. Filter bubbles cannot polarize a society which possesses an ethic of reaching out to understand other perspectives rather than accepting cardboard cut-out renditions of other people. The internet makes this reaching out incredibly easy, if only the will to do so exists.

13. The Importance of Importance

"Nowadays people know the price of everything and the value of nothing."

~Oscar Wilde, *The Picture of Dorian Gray*

We remember what is important to us. We pay attention to what is important to us. We have the self-control to achieve what is important to us. We feel deeply about what is important to us. We can be very clever and creative when we feel it is important to do so.

Yet, when a device *can* do something for us, we no longer *need* to do it ourselves. This seems to strip away importance. Is it inevitable that when outsourcing a skill becomes possible, we no longer value it as a skill?

Historically, this has not been inevitable. In Plato's *Phaedrus*, written at a time when the technology of the written word was starting to be adopted, Socrates criticises dependence on writing because it will encourage people to forget things.[16] Defenders of the unalloyed goodness of digital technologies like to bring this up to show how silly it is to have reservations about the effects a new technology: *hah, old Socrates thought writing was a bad thing! We sure know better now.* What they leave out of this argument is that Socrates is basically right: the written word *can* encourage people to forget things. Literacy enables us to outsource our memories.

Yet, Socrates was not *entirely* right. Literacy may remove the need to remember things that are written down, enabling memory to be outsourced. But it does not inevitably remove the importance of memory altogether. As mentioned in Chapter 11, even after the written word became widespread, memory was valued *for itself*. In the Middle Ages, it came to be considered a cardinal virtue. Those who were literate had the opportunity to outsource their memories, but they generally did not. They sought to further enhance their memories by studying memory as an art.

Why, then, does it *seem* so inevitable that we outsource every skill that we can? To answer this, we have to look at what we prioritize as a culture. People in the Middle Ages believed it was important to store sacred knowledge in their own minds. What about us? What do we value?

> The combination of literacy with memory training may even have allowed for *more* to be remembered than before—the written word brought new sets of symbolic associations into play, which enabled new memory techniques.

Our culture places an extremely high value on 'productivity,' that is, work that is completed as fast as possible. We also place high value on visible, measurable outcomes. These two overlapping priorities explain why, to us, outsourcing our abilities to technology seems like an inevitability rather than a choice.

We tell ourselves we value other things, of course, and indeed many of us put time and effort towards them. But on balance, as a collective, the actions we take tend to show that productivity is really a much higher priority than we might like to think. As mentioned before, actions speak louder than words—even to yourself. The more I act as if working as hard as possible is more important than anything else, the more I build a habit of *feeling* that it is deeply important. This is often encouraged by external pressures, whether of money or workplace culture. Regardless of the cause, it still has the effect of elevating productivity to its current lofty status.

Productivity-prioritising actions are not limited to workplaces. We even seem to approach entertainment with an eye towards productivity, trying to cram as much entertainment into as little time as possible. Schools and learning can receive similar treatment.

Another clue to how important we feel productivity to be is how we use it to justify other things. Even alarm about how the internet affects our minds is often framed in terms of productivity. As part of my research for *Screenfarers*, I searched for and read through popular books about attention and distraction in the digital age. I noticed that most of them are written for professionals who are worried about how they are not getting as much done because they are distracted by checking their notifications constantly, or for managers who are concerned about such behaviour in their employees. Sometimes the goal of productivity is shrouded in the language of 'wellness.' But books which take this angle often emphasize that wellness boosts your productivity, in a way that seems to imply that this represents the true value of health and sanity. *You will have a higher quality of life and more time to smell the flowers*, such a book might say—but such a statement is not quite complete until it is added that *studies show that people who have time to smell the flowers are less stressed and better at focussing on their work.*

This high value we place on productivity is a large part of why it can seem inevitable for cognitive skills to be outsourced to devices. A digital aid which makes a task easier often makes it faster. If tasks can be done faster, we can be more productive. Everyone else is using the faster methods—if we don't keep up, we will no longer be competitive…

There are whole worlds of other values at play in human life which are too often squashed out of the picture in favour of productivity: community, family, generosity, beauty, humour, courage, and gratitude, to name a few. But the value of these is not so easily measured in minutes and dollars. And that brings us to the other quirk of values which makes outsourcing our minds to devices seem like the only option.

In these days of data and statistics, it can be hard to argue for things which are not really measurable. We place a high value on 'evidence' because we place a high value on science. And science is valuable—it is an incredibly useful set of tools for understanding the world. But the thing is, 'evidence' in this sense does not encompass all kinds of evidence, such as the multidimensional evidence of experience. It usually means 'numbers' or 'data.' We are suspicious of experience because it involves bias, so we rely on objective measurement. But by doing so, *we create bias against that which is not measurable.*

We drum the importance of 'evidence' and 'data' into ourselves constantly whenever we communicate information. As a result, that which is measurable feels, somehow, *more real*. It tends to be prioritized in decisions. Partly because, in the light of this constant emphasis, other stuff feels too fluffy and ethereal. Partly because many decisions happen at scale, and these often depend entirely on data to assess their circumstances and track their results—once the scale is too large, experiential evidence isn't even an option because it is too much to experience. The unmeasurable can fall through the cracks, unconsidered. How can you measure fulfillment? Love? Fascination? Character? Virtue? It's easier to stick to productivity—time and dollars and work completed—ignoring all that other stuff.

If we are able to get past this, there are myriad other possible considerations. The question *how can I be as productive as possible?* will almost invariably result in outsourcing a lot of mental abilities—as many as you can. Especially if the competition is doing it. Yet it is possible to ask other questions. *How will this develop my potential? How will this affect my relationships? How will this shape my experience of the world? Is this what I want to be remembered for? Is this something I will look back on fondly?*

Not absolutely necessary does not have to mean *not important*. It is not actually inevitable to abandon skills just because a device can do them for us. But when the priority is to cram as much as possible into every minute, it can seem like a waste of time to puzzle a question out for yourself instead of seeking an instant answer. It can seem pointless to remember things instead of relying on an 'external hard drive.' With so little time, why waste it learning or maintaining a skill when it could be done for you?

There are advantages to developing these skills for oneself, practical and far beyond the practical. Access to the endless possibilities of the human imagination. The ability to synthesize many different pieces of information. The ability to perceive the miraculous in the mundane. We need not only value what is most expedient. It is possible to value skills for themselves, for the experience of using them, and for the ways they enrich our lives.

Socrates' objection to people writing things down and forgetting them was not just about utility. He cared about "the intelligent word graven in the soul of the learner, which can defend itself, and knows when to speak and when to be silent."[17] This is not about forgetting information. It is about losing the experience of living, breathing understanding, "graven in the soul."

Digital technologies allow us to outsource the very skills that create our inner worlds. Skills that imbue life with meaning. Skills that sustain and feed culture. They can't be measured. You can't see them in other people—they are locked up in people's heads. You can only catch glimpses in certain moments. When you are told a story, say, or when you witness a heartfelt performance.

If we find ways to value human skills and not just expedience, these values will not look the same as their Medieval equivalent. We live in a different time, with different competing priorities. Examples from the past cannot solve our problems for us—but they can reveal options we may not otherwise notice. And they can show that what may seem inevitable is not necessarily so.

As individuals, we cannot control the values of our society, nor the economic arrangements they give rise to. Yet we do have the ability to influence what is important to us. Putting time and effort towards something *makes* it important. And individuals who lead by example can inspire more widespread shifts in values.

Many apps now provide suggestions for what you are typing before you type it—Gmail offers entire responses you can send with one click, without needing to respond yourself. Things are getting to the point where our devices are so 'smart' as to hardly need *us*.

Such developments raise a lot of questions about whether being 'more efficient' or 'more productive' is always better. The word 'efficiency' has been employed full-time lately to obscure some important dilemmas of values. "It is more efficient," we say, with the implication that more efficient is obviously better. But nothing is efficient just in general. Efficient at *what*?

In the Industrial Revolution, more efficient typically meant 'takes fewer hours of human effort.' These things were often not more *energy* efficient—human metabolism is much more efficient at converting energy into work than steam engines. Often industrial processes were not even more efficient at meeting human needs—the goal was not to meet needs, but to produce (and sell) as much as possible, vastly exceeding needs for some and leaving others starving in the street.

As we digitize and automate one thing after another, we need to start asking: more efficient at *what*? More efficient at sending natural resources to the landfill in the form of disposable plastic gimmicks? More efficient at eliminating leisure time in favour of constant busyness?

This, in turn, raises questions about the nature and meaning of work. And about what we should do with our lives. Ultimately, the question of the meaning of life cannot be avoided.

Many societies and individuals have grasped for answers to this question and come up with very different things. Should we strive for personal happiness? Monetary success? Elimination of the suffering of others? To take on and fulfill responsibilities? To follow our passions and excel at them? To find contentment with what we have? Towards a more luxurious existence? Should we strive to eliminate the need for work, or work harder, or do work that is more meaningful?

This matter is intimately connected with the issues of persuasive technology. Behaviour design can mean that someone else gets to decide what is 'better,' 'healthier,' 'more efficient.' Persuasive technologies hungry for attention and personal data eat up our time, which *is* our lives. Yet we need not allow the path of least resistance to become the path of least existence.

The question of what we wish to do with our lives is a question of what we wish to do with our time. The answer we have constructed over the last two hundred years is *more of things that are visible and can be measured! More! More! More!*

It's worth taking a step back, and asking: *is this what we really want? What other possibilities exist?*

Part III: Teaching the Art of Screenfaring

14. What Does Success Look Like?

"I am the master of my fate, I am the captain of my soul."

~William Ernest Henley, "Invictus"

What does a skilled screenfarer look like?

A skilled screenfarer knows what they want to accomplish and acts upon it effectively. This might mean wanting to spend time playing video games, while being good at deciding how much is enough and balancing games with other activities. It might mean wanting to not have a cellphone. It might mean spending many hours on screens obsessively learning how to be a programmer, while recognising and dismissing attempts of advertisers or 'user interface candy' to guide one's actions into another activity. Have children and youth set their own goals in this matter whenever possible. That way, they are far more likely to actually put in the effort to develop their skills.

Arguably, many of those who spend countless hours surfing social media aimlessly are 'doing what they want.' How can we define success without being overly prescriptive?

A skilled screenfarer:

- Is deliberate about when, how, for what purpose they use digital technology.
- Is aware of the risks of tech use, and attentive to its mind-shaping effects.
- Monitors the costs of digital interactions against the intended benefits.
- Uses understanding of the psychology of habit-forming design to avoid impigeonment.
- Recognises the futility of the Fear of Missing Out.
- Creates barriers to intentionally contain digital habits.
- Can dismiss opportunities for instant gratification to pursue long-term plans.

The above is the outline of a sort of captain's licence in screenfaring. However, teachers often interact with a particular student for only one year, perhaps even for only one of eight subjects, and have a full curriculum to cover in that limited time.

It is not realistic to expect that the level of screenfaring skill outlined above can be cultivated in a short time. Yet even one lesson can make a substantial difference. Even half an hour spent on this topic can plant the seeds of awareness, concern, and curiosity which may take root and grow on their own.

Here are some more bite-sized goals, which build on each other and constitute progress in the right direction:

1. Students are aware of the pervasive use of habit-forming technology online.
2. Students care about not being manipulated by these techniques.
3. Students have a few tools—both practices and plugins—to resist 'persuasion.'
4. Students pay attention to how much they use devices, and what they spend the time on.
5. Students recognise that their mind and habits are shaped by their experiences.
6. Students habitually recognise 'persuasive' techniques and respond to them consciously.
7. Students can create their own healthy barriers in time and/or space.
8. Students moderate their own tech use based on their tiredness and emotional state.
9. Students have a sense of the possibilities of the mind and value innate human abilities.

Achieving *any* of these, or a few of them, is an excellent aim for lessons and activities which aim to equip students to use digital technology in a balanced and intentional way. Once students are aware there is something happening, they may well manage to make sense of the rest of the situation for themselves, through their own observation and research.

A few cautions around assessment

Assessment can support learning, yet it can also hinder learning. This is, I am sure, well known to teachers reading this. However, the matter of screenfaring gives rise to a few subject-specific assessment pitfalls which are important to keep in mind. These emerge from the very personal nature of screenfaring skills, and from the complexity of our relationship with digital technologies.

One pitfall emerges from the fact that journaling is an effective tool for building reflective awareness, yet digital activities feel like a very private matter. When students log their use of digital technologies, or journal to delve into how these experiences affect them, I recommend that these reflections should be private. If marks must be assigned, they can be simply for completion.

This is because most students will likely not feel comfortable describing all details of their digital activities to their teachers—but for them to develop self-awareness, it is crucial that they have a space to be honest about this with themselves. One way to assess how these activities have affected students would be to have a separate reflection (or discussion) where they are writing explicitly for a teacher and describe what they learned, but can leave out anything they find too personal.

The second pitfall is that it can be hard to draw a sharp line between fact and opinion in the matter of habit-forming technology. And opinions can vary widely on what is acceptable and what is important. I recommend that grades never be assigned for holding specific opinions on issues raised here.

If that happens, instead of grappling with the issues themselves students learn that they should just parrot their teacher's opinion at the right times. For students to care about creating good digital habits, the desire to do so needs to stem from their own values, opinions, understanding, and goals. If they feel opinions are imposed on them, they may be less likely to practice screenfaring skills when no one is enforcing it.

A third, related pitfall, is that I recommend emphasizing thoughtfulness over getting facts correct. Knowing the facts is important in some subjects, and many assessment systems prioritize it. But the key to screenfaring is not knowing the stages of the Hook model, or any other piece of information. What is most important is care, thoughtfulness, paying attention— if those are developed, everything else follows. Guesswork is important for navigating the digital sphere, because in many cases we cannot confirm the 'correct' answer. Why exactly did Facebook put this button here? Chances are, it is not public knowledge. The subject of screenfaring involves scientific information, but it is rather tenuous, shifting, and context-dependent. There are not a lot of things we can say in confident and absolute terms, because experience is so varied. Much of the empirical evidence we have comes from introspection, whether in the form of responses to a psychological survey or personal reflections. This is part of why there isn't a clear line between fact and opinion, as I mention in the previous pitfall.

Self-assessment is a powerful tool for teaching students to take responsibility for their learning. It encourages self-awareness and supports internal motivation, so it is a good match for screenfaring. Having to assess oneself and explain the rationale is difficult and uncomfortable in all the right ways.

In general, I simply advise caution if mixing grades with the subject matter in this book. Grades convey messages about what is important and what is not, based on what they are assigned for. Whatever they make important, however, often can stop being important for itself, but rather for the grade. In school, I dreaded being assigned to study a novel I liked, because being given grades would suck the enjoyment out of it. External rewards can hinder the development of motivation from within. That inner motivation is crucial in the matter of intentional tech use.

With these pitfalls in mind, I leave the rest up to you. You know your students and can gauge when and how to use assessment to best support their learning.

15. Teacher-Parent Co-operation: Creating the Right Conditions

Just as an experienced seafarer would not sail into a raging storm, screenfaring skills can only go so far in adverse conditions.

When I went to university and suddenly had to be on a laptop all day, I was frustrated. I had spent four years offline, examining the internet's impacts on my mind. I understood how it was affecting me. Yet I still had to watch the process happen. My attention span shortened, and it became harder to accomplish things I intended to. I felt less motivated even for things I liked, not to mention homework assignments; I felt like I was dragging myself along, driven by carrots and sticks.

I was more-or-less forced to make a Facebook account, because at my school most events and group projects were organized on that platform. Even official university announcements did not always arrive through other channels. Facebook aside, I was required to check my email frequently to receive information from professors, and had hours of readings each day which were online and not even printable (like interactive e-textbooks with embedded videos).

I tried to establish containing habits. Close any application I am not using, turn my computer off when I am not using it. Only turn the internet connection on when I have a specific purpose in mind. These things would work at first, and then fall apart. I soon realised that everything was set up in ways that made it extremely hard to practice what I was beginning to think of as good attention hygiene. I had to flit between many online platforms to do my assignments, because that was how the assignments were designed. I was constantly tired because of the workload, and so my discipline with closing windows would slip, and my windows would branch and proliferate into a rectilinear jungle.

The point is, to the extent that you are able, *avoid creating conditions that make deliberate tech use harder.* For yourself, your kids, or your students. The two factors most likely to make screenfaring difficult are exhaustion, and unnecessarily requiring the use of digital devices.

Self-control is more difficult when tired. When I am tired, I often fall back on habits. When I am very tired, sometimes I don't even know what I am doing or thinking at the moment, much less what I intended to do in the first place. Constant tiredness makes it very hard to avoid internet rabbitholes or begin to develop the skill of screenfaring. Tiredness can have similar effects to alcohol consumption, slowing cognition and leading to mental lapses.[1] We know that drinking and driving is not a good idea. Trying to create good digital habits while tired is like drinking and then trying to *learn* to drive, except the risks are less obvious and mostly mental.

When one is required to use digital technologies constantly for school or work, it also can be extremely difficult to develop self-control and impose healthy limits. This cannot always be avoided. Many people who work in high-pressure environments will find it hard to change these conditions to enable better screenfaring practices. It may require workplace organizing, and approval from higher-ups, and so on. Awareness of the issue is starting to spread to workplaces, but it might still be an uphill battle.

The good news is that, in the lives of elementary and secondary school students, teachers and parents play a huge role in creating fair weather for screenfaring, or choppy waves. Teachers tend to have a fair bit of say over the format of school assignments. Those which do not specifically require digital tools can be offline. Parents can make choices about what technologies their children have access to, and when. With collaboration and co-ordination *between* teachers and parents, even more can be achieved.

Peer pressure can be a powerful force for good in the matter of digital habits—no one wants to be the one obnoxious person everyone is judging for constantly pulling their phone out.

But at this time, all too often it works the other way: there is a culture of normalcy around unlimited passive tech use and its intrusion into every part of life. Changing this will be much easier with co-ordinated effort! And once the culture shifts, the other aspects of screenfaring and healthy limits become easier.

Speaking to activists who are working to bring more careful consideration to tech use in schools, I learned that sometimes school administrators avoid taking a stand on tech-related issues because they are afraid to create conflict with parents. Yet those very parents may be struggling at home because their child is constantly given digital assignments, and this prevents limits on computer use. Many parents are eager to see schools take initiative. Teachers, administrators, and parents may already agree on what needs to happen—yet without communication, they may fail to act because they do not know they are on the same page!

Teachers and parents can

- Talk with each other about your efforts at home/at school to encourage healthier tech use, how the other party might help support this, and what the situation is like on the other end. Can you co-ordinate rules and limits?
- Talk with your fellow teachers or parents. Seek common ground around what will be best for your children/students. Work together to create a consistent social context that supports healthy limits and deliberate tech use.
- Push back against attempts to introduce 'EdTech' that has not been shown to have benefits. A lot of schools are embracing technologies without carefully vetting them, because they were given free devices or persuaded (without evidence) that a particular app will 'boost test scores.' This can have serious consequences for learning, mental health, privacy, and more. The Screens in Schools Action Kit (see p.123) from the Children's Screentime Action Network is a helpful starting place for organizing around these issues. It is also readily adaptable to the related focus of *Screenfarers* (improving screen time, not just reducing it).

Teachers can

- Avoid assigning digital homework when unnecessary. Most children and youth already spend enormous amounts of time on screens, and it is extremely hard for parents to moderate this. When some of the screen time is for school, it makes matters worse. Plus, reading on paper and writing by hand are beneficial for learning compared to reading on a screen and typing.
- If you assign digital schoolwork, whether as homework or in the classroom, think about the way it is structured in terms of intentional device use. What different applications are involved? What aspects, if any, require internet access? Walk through the project following the "one thing at a time rule" (p. 30). Where might challenges arise? Can you mitigate these, and/or build in principles of good screenfaring?
- Allow for disagreement among students regarding issues of digital technology use. Draw out disagreement and get all sides to consider different perspectives. This way, students are encouraged to think and come to their own conclusions. The conclusions they come to themselves—after some thought and effort—will be more impactful than any that are delivered to them from outside.

Parents can

- Make sure your child is getting enough rest. Avoid over-scheduling their time.
- Create time for unstructured play, and for device-free family activities.
- Let them get bored, pass through boredom, and discover things on the other side.
- Model intentional technology use, and model engaging in other activities.
- Prioritize building trust and encouraging development of self-regulation skills over controlling screen-time and monitoring digital behaviour.
- Entrust children and youth with greater autonomy and responsibility, with the caveat that they must handle it with maturity. This can help the digital not feel like the only place for freedom—when I played videogames as a teenager it was mostly because I didn't have the option of exploring outside and having real-life adventures.
- Ask questions and be curious about your child's perspective on the issue.
- Encourage your child to help remind *you* to use digital technology more deliberately. Make it a household challenge where everyone supports each other.

In ideal screenfaring conditions, the equivalent of a steady breeze, kids and youth are well-rested, well-nourished, have had plenty of physical exercise and in-person social time, their motivation to use their devices intentionally comes from within—from their own goals and dreams, and they trust the adults in their life to help with developing this ability (rather than feeling controlled).

We cannot expect ideal conditions to always be present in life or in screenfaring. However, *the most crucial time for the conditions to be right is when beginning with exercises such as the ones in this book.* Efforts to set kids up for success will go far at this stage. With practice, resistance to adverse conditions can be developed.

16. Food for Critical Thought

One cannot think about behavior design without running up against some—or perhaps all—of the most tangled and messy issues of our time. There are ethical issues and, by extension, legal and regulatory issues. There are conceptual issues. There are issues of values and priorities. All of this makes great material for students to discuss, argue, and disagree over. There really are no easy answers. This can be good, because it makes it possible to draw attention to problems around digital technology without coming off as preachy or controlling. Kids are often primed to resist and become defensive the moment a grown-up starts telling them something negative about digital technology. It is a different matter when you present many sides of the issues and give them the chance to come to their own conclusions.

In the bigger picture, bringing up these topics is a way of including young people in the conversation on matters that profoundly affect their lives. One day, they will be the ones running the companies, making policy decisions, and raising the next generation.

I touch on some of these issues throughout this book. Here is a compilation of some of the key points already raised, along with a few more which did not fit elsewhere. For some topics, I have included links to reading material or videos with various perspectives that students can analyse and compare.

What is technology? What do we mean when we use the word technology? Are there multiple meanings? Is new technology better? What makes a good technology? Do technologies come with a cost? (Introduction, p. 6)

Slot machine or lifesaving resource? Digital media can be addictive for largely the same reasons as slot machines or drugs. But these technologies have myriad benefits that slot machines and drugs do not. For one person they might be a life-threatening habit, for another, a life-saving resource. How can we relate to such a technology? (Chapter 3, p. 40)

What is the difference between punishments and rewards? Are rewards a more humane way to motivate people? Why do we use them? What effects do they have? Can there be too many rewards? What other options are there? (Chapter 3, p. 34)

Does giving people what they want make the world a better place? What happens if is possible for marketers to *create* wants or even needs? What does democracy even mean in this situation? (Chapter 2, p. 24)

What does responsible use of scientific knowledge look like? Are there things we should not even try to control? Are people among them? Where can we draw the ethical lines? When and why is it ethical to try to control people (even if it isn't really 'control')? Scientific knowledge can give us power over things—is that always good? Is it always ethical to create knowledge, knowing that it might be used for controlling or harmful ends? (Chapter 3, p. 35)

What is science? A method for acquiring knowledge? A body of knowledge? An institution made up of people around the world? What are the limits to what science can do? Where can science go wrong? (Chapter 1, p. 14)

What is the meaning of life? What is 'better'? What is 'more efficient'? What things are most important to us? What do we want to do with our lives? When do we want to do things ourselves instead of having them done for us; what is the value of doing something its own sake? (Chapter 13, p. 98)

First Amendment protection for interface design? In US law, the precedent is for computer code to be considered 'speech,' and thus protected under the right for 'free speech.' Free speech may not be forbidden on account of being too persuasive. Is it reasonable to consider habit-forming design merely a form of persuasive speech? If not, why? And where *should* one draw lines between free speech and user interface design? What might the repercussions be of putting that line in different places?

This issue is explored in depth by Kyle Langvardt's award-winning paper "Regulating Habit-Forming Technology." The paper is very long and very academic, but it is also well written and explains the issues with clarity and not too much jargon. It may be worth dipping into with, say, 12th graders in a law class: https://ir.lawnet.fordham.edu/flr/vol88/iss1/4/

How do the numbers crunch for digital advertising? I bring this up with the example of Facebook ads. Students could be assigned to pick a company and look up the information for themselves. Calculations can be done from such information at many different levels of math sophistication, from basic division/multiplication to elaborate algebra. It's a good example of what estimation can reveal.

The numbers I give for ad revenue and users come from this quarterly report which contains other fascinating numbers like profits/person in different regions:
https://s21.q4cdn.com/399680738/files/doc_financials/2020/q3/FB-Q3-2020-Earnings-Presentation.pdf

Sources for approximate click-through rate (CTR) and ad costs:
https://databox.com/average-facebook-ctr#average.
https://fitsmallbusiness.com/how-much-does-facebook-advertising-cost/
https://www.webfx.com/social-media/how-much-does-facebook-advertising-cost.html

This topic can go beyond calculation exercises or making a point about the attention economy. Some proposed solutions to issues around digital tech depend on doing the math. For example, would paying people for their data and time spent looking at ads make the system fairer? Well, how much would someone even be paid? What do the future prospects of the ad-based model for funding the internet look like? Can the current system be sustained for long? What alternatives could there be? Any viable alternative would need to hold up to number crunching! (Chapter 2, p. 26)

Is it really just 'persuasion'? Is there such a thing as 'control' of other people?

> *"The fact is, you can't sell something to people if they don't want that thing. What I'm teaching is persuasion. It is not coercion. Coercion is when you get people to do things they don't want to do. And frankly I don't know how to do that."*
>
> ~Nir Eyal [2]

> *"In the future, there will be two kinds of people in the world: those who let their attention and lives be controlled and coerced by others and those who proudly call themselves 'indistractable.'"*
>
> ~Nir Eyal, *Indistractable* [3]

Spokespeople for persuasive technology insist (sometimes) that they are not coercing anyone. But what is the difference between persuasion and coercion? Can a clear line be drawn at all?

I touch on aspects of the subject in several places: *mind control doesn't exist* (end of Chapter 2, p. 38), *persuasion of individuals vs. groups* (Chapter 3, p. 38), *multiple motivations and 'doing what we already wanted to do'* (Chapter 5, p. 51), *do we have free will? What is free will, exactly?* (Chapter 5, p. 52).

Should there be constraints on advertising and marketing? Why or why not? In what circumstances?

Here is an article on how advertising strategies have evolved, and the subtle ways that advertising works in the internet age. This is written for marketers, not students, but it is an easy read and will help students identify advertising that is not as blatant as a billboard or banner ad:

> https://www.tintup.com/blog/history-evolution-advertising-marketing/

One of the strategies mentioned is providing solutions to problems instead of trying to sell something directly. It is worth noting that these 'solutions' can be effective advertisements even if they do not actually work. The internet is awash with fake how-to videos that show impossible effects, as analysed in the following video (which also touches on the bizarre content farms which have sprung up around the internet, basically huge factories for viral videos):

> *Debunking Fake Videos & WHO'S behind 5-min crafts?*
> https://www.youtube.com/watch?v=pvqa8dsBtno

Who is responsible for addictive technology? And who should do something about it? Should we have self-regulation or legal regulation? I briefly touch on this on page 5, in the introduction, but more elaboration is called for. I have set different perspectives against each other below. Each is part of the ongoing conversation about these dilemmas. At the end there are links to the readings I pulled these perspectives from.

Tristan Harris of the Center for Humane Technology argues that social media companies need to clean up their act—there need to be ethical codes for design which prevent Big Tech from exploiting our fragile brain wiring.

Nir Eyal argues that it is not the technology that distracts us—distractions come from within, and even without devices we will find ways to distract ourselves. But we have the power to learn to be "Indistractible."

Harris says that putting the responsibility on individuals for this is dangerous—a free pass for tech companies whose irresponsible use of behavioural psychology is eroding democracy and 'downgrading' our minds. Giving responsibility to the individuals would be blaming the victim.

Facebook and other huge tech firms have been taking some of Harris's advice on board, apparently starting to 'optimize' for "Time Well Spent," a slogan of the Centre for Humane Technology. This sounds like an improvement on the previous goal of 'time on device.' In a long-form journalism piece for the Guardian, Ben Tarnoff and Moira Weigel argue that this move—although good for PR—may actually just make Facebook *more* profit, by helping them collect better, more detailed data on what each person *really* cares about, improving the value of the data they sell to advertisers. In fact, past attempts to 'humanize' technology seem to have actually *created* its current invasion into every corner of modern life.

If neither Silicon Valley nor individuals can be expected to solve the problem, should governments step in? How could this be done in a way that respects civic freedoms and is not heavy-handed?

Digital technologies remove many barriers, and this can create complicated dilemmas. I have discussed earlier how they can remove barriers between one activity and another—they also remove barriers between kinds of media: music, videos, text, social media, and more all intertwine. They create the potential for tech companies to easily adapt around regulations and sprout out of loopholes, far faster than thoughtful regulations could hope to be produced. In an article called "If the internet is addictive, why don't we regulate it?" Michael Schulson writes:

> *"The designer drug market provides a helpful analogy here. Every time governments ban these substances—which include synthetic cannabinoids, often called K2 or Spice—designers simply come out with a new, slightly different version that slips through the strictures of the law. Similarly, with something as slippery as distraction, and as polymorphous as the web, it's easy to imagine companies finding ways to tweak their designs and find new ways to hook users."* [4]

Many of the big voices speaking out about problems with persuasive technology are Silicon Valley insiders. Tristan Harris co-founded Instagram. He and Nir Eyal both studied persuasive design under B.J. Fogg. On one hand, this means they have an inside perspective, and they have a lot of credibility in drawing attention to issues around tech use. On the other, it means they think about the issues in the same way as the people who helped create the issues in the first place—indeed, as with Harris and Eyal, they often *are* those people.

The Center for Humane Technology is one example of this. Another is an AI company called Boundless Mind which made an app called Space to help people curb their phone addiction (by using algorithms that track them). An old website for Space that was taken down recently boasted "We use AI and neuroscience to find the perfect moment of zen to give you. It's the same math that we use to get people addicted to apps, just run backwards." According to the Space app site, people have "no way to fight back" against addictive tech, and "they can't *actually*…delete the apps." (see below for a link to the archived site.)

What does each of these angles contribute? Is there a middle ground between victim blaming and giving up all personal responsibility? Should those who have created a problem be responsible for resolving it? Are they capable of doing so? How does a company's need to turn a profit interact with ethics? What voices are missing from this conversation?

Here are some great sources to use with teens as a basis for discussing the tangle, and to examine some very interesting rhetoric:

Suggested readings:

Perspectives of Eyal and Harris side-by-side (top-down vs personal responsibility):

Addicted to Screens? That's a You Problem
https://www.nytimes.com/2019/10/06/technology/phone-screen-addiction-tech-nir-eyal.html

Ben Tarnoff and Moira Weigel on how tech companies may profit at our expense while seeming 'more humane:'

Why Silicon Valley Can't Fix Itself
https://www.theguardian.com/news/2018/may/03/why-silicon-valley-cant-fix-itself-tech-humanism

Michael Schulson argues for the importance of regulation of addictive design, while also revealing some of the roadblocks:

If the Internet is Addictive, Why Don't We Regulate It?
https://aeon.co/essays/if-the-internet-is-addictive-why-don-t-we-regulate-it

The following video discusses issues with regulating 'loot boxes' in video games under gambling laws (the main approach currently being considered), explained by a gamer and game designer. The points raised go beyond video games to all digital applications of 'hook'-like strategies and the issues with regulating them:

The Legality of Loot Boxes - Designing Ethical Lootboxes: II
https://www.youtube.com/watch?v=26ZX7NbOhks

A fascinating rhetoric case study from the company Boundless Mind:

Boundless Mind (originally called Dopamine Labs) becomes Thrive Global (all the same company) and the rhetoric goes from incredibly brash to gentle and wellness-oriented. Worth comparing, as the difference is spectacular:

https://web.archive.org/web/20191008195050/https:/www.boundless.ai/

https://web.archive.org/web/20201007232128/https://thriveglobal.com/

Old website for the Space app by Boundless Mind (not sure if I should say it is disturbing or entertaining, but presumably it was taken down for being a PR disaster. Too honest, perhaps?):

http://web.archive.org/web/20191209102045/http://www.youjustneedspace.com/

One of the founders of the company describes and defends 'Brain Hacking' (5 min video):

https://www.youtube.com/watch?v=TzDDpT11O_A

These are some of the big questions and interesting readings I have come across while writing this book. There are doubtless many more. You likely already have questions of your own, and the children in our lives may bring up questions neither you nor I had thought of before. The material here is just a starting point; the potential for exploration is limitless.

17. Directions for the Future

At the present time, digital technologies are an extremely new phenomenon in human experience. We have not yet formed cultural habits and norms that allow us to deal with them responsibly. Lacking these, our whole society is still in a period of reckless adolescent indulgence.

I created this book to help fill a gap in resources addressing the specifics of how digital interactions shape the mind and what we can do about it. This first edition was written for individual teachers and parents who want to address issues around habit-forming technology, impigeonment, and outsourcing, but do not yet have support from schoolboards to do so. The content and exercises are intended to be as adaptable as possible, so that whether you are teaching a third-grade class, or twelfth-grade science, or middle school history, screenfaring guidance and information about the psychology behind digital interfaces can be woven in with the subject matter you are already teaching.

The aim of *Screenfarers* goes well beyond the first edition, however. This project is a step towards creating the three conditions necessary for large-scale education towards healthier tech-use habits:

1. Effective resources must be available.

2. The effectiveness of these resources must be demonstrable.

3. The importance of the topic must be recognized by authorities such as school boards and education ministers.

As you try out exercises and ideas in this book, there is a lot you can do to contribute to all three of these goals. By giving feedback on what has worked, what could be improved, and how you have adapted *Screenfarers* to your particular circumstances, you can help build a knowledge base around how to equip young people to navigate the strange, virtual, parallel reality we have created.

Feedback from teachers and parents is not only helpful for improvement, it also is valuable as evidence of what works. For now, qualitative feedback can be the evidence of success; in future, I plan to work with survey design and data experts to build ways of collecting and pooling quantitative as well as qualitative data on results.

Qualitative and quantitative data collected on the benefits of screenfaring education would also contribute further to building a case for its importance. So does creating and using language that allows us to more clearly diagnose problems with 'persuasive technology.' Teacher and parent advocacy is also key for ensuring top-down efforts to address these issues.

Once all three conditions are fulfilled, we can expect to see public education systems find ways to better prepare students to deal with the digital worlds they are surrounded by. Imagine if a whole generation was aware of the attention economy, the psychology behind habit-forming interfaces, and how to interact with such things thoughtfully. Digital platforms would largely lose their power to have unwanted effects on us.

Designers of digital platforms who seek to make their products as addictive as possible do not pass through a meticulous peer review process. They make an educated guess about what might work, try out some different versions, collect data on what seems to most effectively increase 'time on device,' and then scale up the most successful attempts. This method of iterative tweaking and testing is part of what is behind the extremely rapid evolution of digital interfaces. In order to respond effectively to these rapid changes, I propose that we borrow from this approach.

This book is far from perfect. The situation it describes is in flux, with constant new developments that no one person could hope to keep track of. I have limited experience as a teacher, and almost none of it in a classroom. I am not a parent—anything I know about parenting comes from conversations with my parents, friends who are parents, and my fairly recent experience of being a child. This book, though based on years of experience and research, is essentially my educated guess.

With a community effort, however, the ideas I present here can be built upon, improved, and cross-pollinated with other approaches. Through feedback from teachers, parents, children, and youth, through discussion and collaboration, we can pool our intelligence and experience. We can find what works and share it around. It may be a bit harder to measure screenfaring ability than 'time on device,' but I believe that if teachers and parents who are facing these challenges work together, we will learn and discover an immense amount. Silicon Valley startups may have more money and data, but that is no match for the collective experience of teachers and parents around the world. We vastly outnumber them. And direct experience generates far more nuanced information than tracking algorithms.

One of the core messages of this book is how crucial it is to *observe*. So, my invitation is this: do not take my claims at face value. See for yourself if they work. Tweak them to serve you better, and to better fit your particular situation. Then share your discoveries, so they can be a resource to others as we collectively grapple with a difficult problem.

For the moment, the best place to send feedback, criticism, successes, and ideas is the contact form at screenfarers.com. I also plan to add a forum to the website so there can be discussion instead of only centralized communication. If there is no forum yet, and you are keen for one, let me know via the feedback form and I will hurry up my forum-building!

According to reports from Common Sense Media, US children age 0 to 8 spend an average of two and a half hours on screen media per day—a quarter of them spend four hours or more.[5] 8-to-12-year-olds spend about five hours on screens per day, and teens average about seven and a half.[6] These numbers do not even include screen time related to schoolwork. How can screen time be taking a similar chunk of the day to *sleep*? And that was *before* the COVID-19 measure of digitalizing everything.

"Screen time" in itself is, as I've mentioned in previous chapters, not the most helpful metric. It matters what one is doing exactly. It seems clear, however, that the majority of internet activity (across all ages) is not thoughtful or deliberate. It is less following an inner compass of what we want to spend time on, and more being lured hither and thither by various multimedia carrots—practicing and mastering a form of constant distraction which carries over into non-digital life.

As widespread understanding of this strange collective experience emerges, we *will* develop norms, traditions, social arrangements, and skills that allow us the benefits of digital connection while neither sacrificing our other abilities, nor being led around unconsciously till we become the product that is sold.

Schools are one of the most crucial places for building awareness of the issues around how we relate to digital technologies at present. They are also essential for laying the foundations from which a new relationship will emerge. We have a grand challenge before us as a society. I hope this book will contribute a few useful tools.

Acknowledgements

This book would not have been possible without the help of many friends, mentors, and family members. Sam Hollon collaborated with me on the initial research project that snowballed into this book. Bits of his ideas and research have made their way in here, and our conversations over the years have been invaluable to my thinking around the subject. Nicki Rehn and Natalie Bursztyn generously suffered through the crude initial draft which became *Screenfarers*. Their feedback greatly helped guide it into its final form. Kathryn Neely used her librarian powers to help me with research conundrums and technical difficulties. Zach DeWitt read and reread my drafts and told me what I was doing wrong—the book is far better for it. Our discussions helped me figure out what I was actually trying to say in many a muddled bit of manuscript. Carl Natiuk read and reread my drafts and told me what I was doing right. He helped with every stage of editing, from early structural problems to final proofreads. He also put up with months of me consulting him at random moments when I felt stuck, and patiently saw me through various formatting emergencies. Gerhardt Troan helped me hunt down typos and gnarled sentences.

My parents encouraged me to develop my writing from an early age, raised me in a television-free house filled with all kinds of strange and interesting books, and taught me to ask questions. They supported my efforts in writing this book, providing feedback and insights along the way. They also put up with the experiments from which I draw my experience—for instance, years of receiving only handwritten letters, in an era when other parents expect responses to texts.

The natural habitats of questions and of imagination are endangered these days, and I am fortunate to have been immersed in them. I am indebted to quiet, and to long walks in the woods. To the children I work with, who never cease to inspire. Their endless playfulness, their fascination with the world, and their joy in learning are contagious. And a reminder of what we need to protect.

List of Common Behaviour Design Features

Pull-to-refresh, followed by 'loading' wheel—used by Twitter, though also found elsewhere, this design loads new tweets, emails, or messages when you tug on the smartphone screen. Neither the 'loading' delay nor the 'pull' are technically necessary. They are there only to build anticipation and create a habit of actively checking what new things might show up.

Infinite scroll, a.k.a. the 'bottomless bowl'—this is widespread in search results, timelines, newsfeeds, and similar structures (every company helpfully calls them something different). It is facing pushback for its relatively obvious drawbacks of encouraging people to scroll for hours, losing track of time; whether having interruptions in the scroll will be less impigeonating remains to be seen.

Staggered pictures—on Pinterest, photos are staggered instead of in rows, so that you always see parts of the next few photos, get curious about them, and keep scrolling.

Autoplay—this is the infinite scroll of the video world. The next video, even if you don't want to watch it, often has a few seconds to get you interested before you can stop it from playing. For very young children, on platforms like YouTube Kids, often autoplay algorithmically selects one video after another and keeps running with no input from the child.

Suggestions and clickbait—many websites, including YouTube, Facebook, Amazon, nearly all news websites, and those weird 'top ten' list sites, show viewers algorithmically-suggested related content, with catchy headlines calculated to inspire curiosity, or intriguing pictures, etc. The idea is to get people to click on these and keep reading/watching. Often ads and sponsored links are discreetly mixed in.

Like button, and other social reactions/rating systems—this enables users of a platform to give each other 'variable rewards' that don't feel as arbitrary as algorithmically generated ones because they come from people.

Notifications—notification icons (generally coloured red to grab attention) encourage you to check what has happened and to feel like there are always things to keep up with. Sometimes the notifications do not have much to do with you, for example, Facebook recommending people for you to 'friend,' but notifications can still create a thrill of anticipation, and it's easy to get in the habit of following up on all of them before doing what you actually meant to do.

Daily streak—on Snapchat, the gamification element of 'daily streaks' for messaging someone on Snapchat for multiple days in a row encourages regular use. One can see how, between young friends, keeping up a 'streak' can be interpreted as a gesture of friendship and commitment. Similar 'streak' mechanisms are used in other platforms.

Achievements—giving 'badges' and 'level-ups' for various metrics is common in many social and educational platforms, and I have even seen it used in forums. These could be for using the platform for a year, watching a certain number of lessons, posting a certain number of times, receiving a certain number of responses, and so on. Sometimes these achievements are publicly visible, lending credibility and status to the achiever.

Loot boxes—a mechanic used in many video games. Players receive random items when they open a 'loot box' (or, say, defeat an enemy). Sometimes loot boxes need to be paid for, and paid ones can contain exclusive items superior to what is available for free. These are thoroughly based on the idea of variable rewards, and critics of the mechanic compare it to gambling (though, unlike traditional gambling, you cannot generally win real currency).

Bait and Switch—Instagram recently swapped out their notification button for a shopping icon, so that people habitually accustomed to using the button to see the activity of their friends now have their attention drawn to shopping instead (and have to go find the other button elsewhere).[7] Indeed, this will likely be sufficient for many people to click the shop button out of habit and then see something that they like before they realise their mistake.

These are examples, but with thousands of platforms out there trying to come up with their own habit-forming designs, it is crucial to have the self-awareness to recognise the principles of habit-forming technology in new forms. Not all behaviour designs are icons one can pick out easily.

The sneakiest designs are the ones that seem to emerge naturally from a combination of different things. These are the hardest to notice or name. The easiest way to detect subtler designs may be how you feel after using a platform, and how it influences what you want to do. This is part of why *Screenfarers* includes exercises for both awareness of interface design and of one's personal experience of the feelings it creates. One cannot guarantee that these experiences are always the intended ones—but assuming they are is a useful place to start, considering that we cannot necessarily know what is going on behind the scenes. On a personal level it doesn't matter what was intended—noticing the effects something has on *you* allows you to take steps to tweak those effects if you choose.

Resource List

While writing this book, I came across various things which may be helpful for teaching the subject, and related subjects. I have included them here in case they are of use.

Initiatives, Advocacy, and Resource Collections

Screens in Schools Action Kit

https://commercialfreechildhood.org/pf/sis-kit-2020/

These free resources support teachers and parents in advocating for tech use in schools to be incorporated *only when it has educational merit*—instead of when tech companies have been very effective at *claiming* their products have educational merit. This is a much-needed complement to the Screenfarers approach, especially where classrooms are packed with 'EdTech.'

The resources combine action steps, letter templates, and similar guidance with descriptions of the mental, physical, and emotional harms that result from excessive digital technology use. These descriptions cite research extensively and are specifically framed so that teachers and parents can use the information to advocate for a more carefully considered approach to tech in education. I highly recommend these resources as a supplement to this book.

The Action Kit includes a COVID-19-specific addendum. Another COVID resource list:

https://commercialfreechildhood.org/pf/covid-rec-resources/

The "EdTech Triangle" from Everyschool

https://everyschool.org/the-edtech-triangle

This is a research-based framework for evaluating whether a technology is worth introducing as an educational tool or not.

Wait until 8th

https://www.waituntil8th.org/

Wait until 8th provides a way for parents at the same school to pledge to not allow their children to own a smartphone until at least 8th grade. It is a tool for helping shift the social dynamic, removing peer pressure around smartphones by co-ordinating with other parents, and to keep smartphones out of primary schools. We need more ways to organise collectively like this!

Educator Toolkit for Teacher and Student Privacy (US-specific): https://www.studentprivacymatters.org/educator-toolkit-for-teacher-and-student-privacy/

Parent Toolkit for Student Privacy (US-specific): https://www.studentprivacymatters.org/toolkit/

Advertising and Consumerism

The Propaganda Game

The board game "Propaganda" can be a fun way to teach students to recognise tricks employed in advertising and other media. It also has a digital version, specifically set up to be usable by teachers:
> https://propagandagame.org
> https://boardgamegeek.com/boardgame/5647/propaganda-game

Two different perspectives for students to read on the history of consumerism and work: https://orionmagazine.org/article/the-gospel-of-consumption/

https://www.theatlantic.com/business/archive/2016/11/how-humans-became-consumers/508700/

The Story of Stuff

Widespread use of habit-forming techniques online is incentivised by ad money. But for there to be advertising, people need to be buying things. These short videos (appropriate for all ages) take an environmental angle on consumer culture and the impacts of our production and use of "stuff:"

The Story of Stuff: https://www.storyofstuff.org/movies/story-of-stuff/
The Story of Electronics: https://www.storyofstuff.org/movies/story-of-electronics/
The Story of Citizens United v. FEC [How corporations are interacting with democracy]:
> https://www.storyofstuff.org/story-of-citizens-united-v-fec/

Skills and Non-Digital Experiences

Memory

Memory Craft by Lynne Kelly (2019) brings together memory techniques from cultures around the world and presents them in order from simplest to most complex. The book is written so that you can follow along and try things out yourself. This is the best book I have come across for learning and teaching the art of memory.

Tons of free memory resources can be found at https://artofmemory.com/. The site has e-courses, a wiki, and specific advice for different kinds of memorization.

Outdoor Classrooms as COVID-19 response

National COVID-19 Outdoor Learning Initiative:
https://www.greenschoolyards.org/covid-learn-outside

The Case for Outdoor School During and After COVID (including resources to get started):
https://durablehuman.com/the-case-for-outdoor-learning-during-and-after-covid/

Guide to Advocating for Outdoor Classrooms in Coronavirus-Era School Reopening:
https://www.nwf.org/-/media/Documents/PDFs/NWF-Reports/2020/COVID-19-Outdoor-Classroom-Policy-Guide

Nature Education and Naturalist Skills

Children and Nature Network resource collection:
https://www.childrenandnature.org/resource-hub/resources/

Vitamin N: The Essential Guide to a Nature-Rich Life by Richard Louv (2016) is the practical companion to his book *Last Child in the Woods*, where he coined the term 'Nature Deficit Disorder:'
http://richardlouv.com/books/vitamin-n/

Coyote's Guide to Connecting with Nature by Jon Young, Ellen Haas, and Evan McGown (2010). This book is packed with activities which are designed to facilitate nature connection and experiential learning about the natural world, in a way that is playful and cultivates curiosity:
https://www.wildernessawareness.org/store/alumni-authored/coyotes-guide-to-connecting-with-nature-2nd-edition/

What the Robin Knows: How Birds Reveal the Secrets of the Natural World by Jon Young (2013) is a guide to learning to understand the signals birds send each other—a skill kids delight in once they discover its existence: http://birdlanguage.com/products/what-the-robin-knows/

Tracking and the Art of Seeing: how to read animal tracks and sign by Paul Rezendes (1999) is one of the best tracking books I have come across. It goes into far more detail on the different kinds of sign to look for than most (including dens, for example). There are lots of other good books on animal tracking out there, though, and time carefully observing the natural world is the most important aspect of learning the skill.

> The slam poem "Ordinary Powers" by Christian Drake is a fun source of inspiration:
>
> https://www.youtube.com/watch?v=zAepucMM

Making Things

https://www.instructables.com/

Instructables is a great source of project ideas and instructions for making things. Anyone can create their own instructables, too, and there are frequently contests, some of which are specifically for students.

Recommended Academic Works

The three most valuable pieces of academic writing I have found in this realm. Each of these takes a different angle, and each is a major nexus of other research, citing hundreds of sources.

Loh, Kep Kee, and Ryota Kanai. 'How Has the Internet Reshaped Human Cognition?' *The Neuroscientist* 22, no. 5 (October 2016): 506–20. https://doi.org/10.1177/1073858415595005.

Langvardt, Kyle. 'Regulating Habit-Forming Technology'. *SSRN Electronic Journal*, 2019. https://doi.org/10.2139/ssrn.3351936.

Lyngs, Ulrik, Kai Lukoff, Petr Slovak, Reuben Binns, Adam Slack, Michael Inzlicht, Max Van Kleek, and Nigel Shadbolt. 'Self-Control in Cyberspace: Applying Dual Systems Theory to a Review of Digital Self-Control Tools'. In *Proceedings of the 2019 CHI Conference on Human Factors in Computing Systems - CHI '19*, 1–18. Glasgow, UK: ACM Press, 2019. https://doi.org/10.1145/3290605.3300361.

(The normal DOI link above is paywalled, but Lyngs makes the PDF available for free on his website, here: https://ulriklyngs.com/publications/)

Stuart McMillen Comics

Stuart McMillen has created several thought provoking webcomics on tech/media issues:
http://www.stuartmcmillen.com/comic/defending-dumbphones/
http://www.stuartmcmillen.com/comic/first-got-the-internet/

And this one on the nature of drug addiction is indirectly relevant to tech addiction:
http://www.stuartmcmillen.com/comic/rat-park/

Videos about Videogames

The following videos address ethics, monetization, and regulation of videogames from the perspective of a game designer. These videos are aimed at other game designers, but are pretty concisely explained with cartoony graphics. For kids who play a lot of video games, the angle is helpful: it doesn't sound like alarmism or 'video games bad.' The narrator *is* a gamer, and discusses psychological tricks in games, the difference between 'skinner boxes' and real enjoyment, how games are or should be monetized, and the tangled issues with applying gambling laws to games (issues that apply well beyond the video game world).

Doing Free to Play Wrong - How Bad Monetization Harms F2P Games
https://www.youtube.com/watch?v=Mhz9OXy86a0

Free to Play Is Currently Broken - How High Costs Drive Players Away from F2P Games
https://www.youtube.com/watch?v=FwI0u9L4R8U

The Loot Box Question - Designing Ethical Lootboxes: I
https://www.youtube.com/watch?v=-Uha5c7hJdA

The Legality of Loot Boxes - Designing Ethical Lootboxes: II
https://www.youtube.com/watch?v=26ZX7NbOhks

As I continue reading and learning and speaking to people about these issues, I will no doubt learn of additional resources and my list of recommendations will change. In addition, some of the links in the list above may break over time.

For an updated resource list, check out screenfarers.com/resources.

Bibliography

Abram, David. *The Spell of the Sensuous: Perception and Language in a More-Than-Human World*. New York: Pantheon Books, 1996.

Azrin, N. H., and R. G. Nunn. 'Habit-Reversal: A Method of Eliminating Nervous Habits and Tics'. *Behaviour Research and Therapy* 11, no. 4 (November 1973): 619–28. https://doi.org/10.1016/0005-7967(73)90119-8.

Bate, Karina S., John M. Malouff, Einar T. Thorsteinsson, and Navjot Bhullar. 'The Efficacy of Habit Reversal Therapy for Tics, Habit Disorders, and Stuttering: A Meta-Analytic Review'. *Clinical Psychology Review* 31, no. 5 (July 2011): 865–71. https://doi.org/10.1016/j.cpr.2011.03.013.

Bowles, Nellie. 'Addicted to Screens? That's Really a You Problem (Published 2019)'. *The New York Times*, 6 October 2019, sec. Technology. https://www.nytimes.com/2019/10/06/technology/phone-screen-addiction-tech-nir-eyal.html.

Burke, James. *Connections*. 1st American ed. Boston: Little, Brown and Company, 1978.

Clausen, Meredith L. 'The Department Store: Development of the Type'. *Journal of Architectural Education* 39, no. 1 (1985): 20–29.

Davis, Kathleen. 'A (Kind of) Brief History of Marketing (Infographic)'. Entrepreneur, 17 July 2013. https://www.entrepreneur.com/article/227438.

Davis, Wade. 'Dreams from Endangered Cultures'. TED. Accessed 28 November 2020. https://www.ted.com/talks/wade_davis_dreams_from_endangered_cultures.

———. *Light at the Edge of the World: A Journey Through the Realm of Vanishing Cultures*. Fourth Impression edition. Vancouver: Douglas & McIntyre, 2007.

———. *The Wayfinders: Why Ancient Wisdom Matters in the Modern World*. First Edition. Toronto: House of Anansi Press, 2009.

Edwards, Haley Sweetland. 'Silicon Valley Knows How to Program Human Behavior—for Better or Worse'. *Time*, 23 April 2018.

Engber, Daniel. 'Everything Is Crumbling'. *Slate*, 6 March 2016. http://www.slate.com/articles/health_and_science/cover_story/2016/03/ego_depletion_an_influential_theory_in_psychology_may_have_just_been_debunked.html.

Eyal, Nir. *Hooked: How to Build Habit-Forming Products*. Edited by Ryan Hoover. Rev. ed. New York, New York: Portfolio, 2014.

———. *Indistractable: How to Control Your Attention and Choose Your Life*. Dallas, TX: BenBella Books, 2019.

Ferster, C. B., and B. F. Skinner. *Schedules of Reinforcement*. Cambridge, Massachusetts: B.F. Skinner Foundation, 2014.

Feynman, Richard P. *The Pleasure of Finding Things Out: The Best Short Works of Richard Feynman*. Cambridge, Massachusetts: Perseus Books, 1999.

Fogg, B. J. 'About BJ Fogg, PhD Behaviour Scientist at Stanford University'. BJ Fogg, PhD. Accessed 12 October 2020. https://www.bjfogg.com/about.

———. 'Persuasive Computers: Perspectives and Research Directions'. In *Proceedings of the SIGCHI Conference on Human Factors in Computing Systems - CHI '98*, 225–32. Los Angeles, California, United States: ACM Press, 1998. https://doi.org/10.1145/274644.274677.

———. *Persuasive Technology: Using Computers to Change What We Think and Do.* 1 edition. Amsterdam; Boston: Morgan Kaufmann, 2002.

———. *Tiny Habits: The Small Changes That Change Everything*. Illustrated Edition. Boston: Houghton Mifflin Harcourt, 2019.

Gallegos, Jose Angelo. 'The History and Evolution of Advertising'. *The TINT Blog* (blog), 30 June 2016. https://www.tintup.com/blog/history-evolution-advertising-marketing/.

Quote Investigator. 'Google Can Bring You Back 100,000 Answers. A Librarian Can Bring You Back the Right One'. Accessed 24 November 2020. https://quoteinvestigator.com/2016/04/23/library/.

He, Qinghua, Ofir Turel, and Antoine Bechara. 'Brain Anatomy Alterations Associated with Social Networking Site (SNS) Addiction'. *Scientific Reports* 7, no. 1 (23 March 2017): 45064. https://doi.org/10.1038/srep45064.

Hern, Alex. 'Netflix's Biggest Competitor? Sleep'. *The Guardian*, 18 April 2017, sec. Technology. https://www.theguardian.com/technology/2017/apr/18/netflix-competitor-sleep-uber-facebook.

Hollister, Sean. 'Mattel Is Making an Amazon Echo That Understands Your Kids, Too'. CNET. Accessed 28 October 2020. https://www.cnet.com/reviews/aristotle-by-nabi-preview/.

Horvath, Juliane, Christina Mundinger, Mike M. Schmitgen, Nadine D. Wolf, Fabio Sambataro, Dusan Hirjak, Katharina M. Kubera, Julian Koenig, and Robert Christian Wolf. 'Structural and Functional Correlates of Smartphone Addiction'. *Addictive Behaviors* 105 (1 June 2020): 106334. https://doi.org/10.1016/j.addbeh.2020.106334.

TechCrunch. 'Instagram Swaps out Its "Activity" Tab for "Shop" in New Global Test'. Accessed 28 November 2020. https://social.techcrunch.com/2020/07/07/instagram-swaps-out-its-activity-tab-for-shop-in-new-global-test/.

Kelly, Lynne. *Knowledge and Power in Prehistoric Societies: Orality, Memory and the Transmission of Culture.* New York: Cambridge University Press, 2015.

———. *Memory Craft: Improve Your Memory Using the Most Powerful Methods from around the World*, 2019.

Kühn, Simone, and Jürgen Gallinat. 'Brains Online: Structural and Functional Correlates of Habitual Internet Use: Correlates of Internet Use'. *Addiction Biology* 20, no. 2 (March 2015): 415–22. https://doi.org/10.1111/adb.12128.

Kurniasanti, Kristiana Siste, Pratiwi Assandi, Raden Irawati Ismail, Martina Wiwie Setiawan Nasrun, and Tjhin Wiguna. 'Internet Addiction: A New Addiction?' *Medical Journal of*

Indonesia 28, no. 1 (8 May 2019): 82–91. https://doi.org/10.13181/mji.v28i1.2752.

Kuss, Daria Joanna, and Mark D. Griffiths. 'Internet Gaming Addiction: A Systematic Review of Empirical Research'. *International Journal of Mental Health and Addiction* 10, no. 2 (1 April 2012): 278–96. https://doi.org/10.1007/s11469-011-9318-5.

Langvardt, Kyle. 'Regulating Habit-Forming Technology'. *SSRN Electronic Journal*, 2019. https://doi.org/10.2139/ssrn.3351936.

Lebow, Victor. 'Price Competition in 1955'. *Journal of Retailing*, Spring 1955.

Lin, Xiao, Guangheng Dong, Qiandong Wang, and Xiaoxia Du. 'Abnormal Gray Matter and White Matter Volume in "Internet Gaming Addicts"'. *Addictive Behaviors* 40 (1 January 2015): 137–43. https://doi.org/10.1016/j.addbeh.2014.09.010.

Liu, Ang, and Tian Meng Li. 'Develop Habit-Forming Products Based on the Axiomatic Design Theory'. *Procedia CIRP* 53 (2016): 119–24. https://doi.org/10.1016/j.procir.2016.07.035.

Loh, Kep Kee, and Ryota Kanai. 'How Has the Internet Reshaped Human Cognition?' *The Neuroscientist* 22, no. 5 (October 2016): 506–20. https://doi.org/10.1177/1073858415595005.

Lyngs, Ulrik. 'What I Hate, That Do I: Religion as a Cultural Tool for Cognitive Control'. MA dissertation, Aarhus University, 2016.

Lyngs, Ulrik, Kai Lukoff, Petr Slovak, Reuben Binns, Adam Slack, Michael Inzlicht, Max Van Kleek, and Nigel Shadbolt. 'Self-Control in Cyberspace: Applying Dual Systems Theory to a Review of Digital Self-Control Tools'. In *Proceedings of the 2019 CHI Conference on Human Factors in Computing Systems - CHI '19*, 1–18. Glasgow, UK: ACM Press, 2019. https://doi.org/10.1145/3290605.3300361.

Marty-Dugas, Jeremy, Brandon C. W. Ralph, Jonathan M. Oakman, and Daniel Smilek. 'The Relation between Smartphone Use and Everyday Inattention.' *Psychology of Consciousness: Theory, Research, and Practice* 5, no. 1 (March 2018): 46–62. https://doi.org/10.1037/cns0000131.

Matthews, Dona. 'Why Parents Really Need to Put Down Their Phones'. Psychology Today. Accessed 14 November 2020. https://www.psychologytoday.com/blog/going-beyond-intelligence/201711/why-parents-really-need-put-down-their-phones.

Miller, Michael B. *The Bon Marché: Bourgeois Culture and the Department Store, 1869-1920*. Princeton, New Jersey: Princeton University Press, 1981.

Paulus, Martin P., Lindsay M. Squeglia, Kara Bagot, Joanna Jacobus, Rayus Kuplicki, Florence J. Breslin, Jerzy Bodurka, et al. 'Screen Media Activity and Brain Structure in Youth: Evidence for Diverse Structural Correlation Networks from the ABCD Study'. *NeuroImage* 185 (15 January 2019): 140–53. https://doi.org/10.1016/j.neuroimage.2018.10.040.

Plato. 'Phaedrus'. The Internet Classics Archive. Accessed 18 November 2019. http://classics.mit.edu/Plato/phaedrus.html.

Putnam, Robert D. *Bowling Alone: Revised and Updated: The Collapse and Revival of*

American Community. Simon and Schuster, 2020.

Ramsay Brown, Boundless Mind at The Montgomery Summit 2018. MontyTV, 2018. https://www.youtube.com/watch?v=TzDDpT11O_A.

Rideout, V., and M. B. Robb. 'The Common Sense Census: Media Use by Kids Age Zero to Eight, 2020'. San Francisco, CA: Common Sense Media, 2020. https://www.commonsensemedia.org/sites/default/files/uploads/research/2020_zero_to_eight_census_final_web.pdf.

———. 'The Common Sense Census: Media Use by Tweens and Teens, 2019'. San Francisco, CA: Common Sense Media, 2019. https://www.commonsensemedia.org/sites/default/files/uploads/research/2019-census-8-to-18-full-report-updated.pdf.

Schulson, Michael. 'If the Internet Is Addictive, Why Don't We Regulate It?' Aeon. Accessed 2 October 2020. https://aeon.co/essays/if-the-internet-is-addictive-why-don-t-we-regulate-it.

Shirky, Clay. 'Gin, Television, and Social Surplus'. *Here Comes Everybody* (blog), 2 January 2011. https://web.archive.org/web/20110102193349/http://www.shirky.com/herecomeseverybody/2008/04/looking-for-the-mouse.html.

Tarnoff, Ben, and Moira Weigel. 'Why Silicon Valley Can't Fix Itself'. *The Guardian*, 3 May 2018, sec. News. https://www.theguardian.com/news/2018/may/03/why-silicon-valley-cant-fix-itself-tech-humanism.

Williamson, Ann, and R. Friswell. 'Fatigue and Driving: Disentangling the Relative Effects of Time of Day and Sleep Deprivation', 7. Adelaide, South Australia: University of New South Wales, 2008.

Wisehart, M. K. 'Making Your Imagination Work for You'. *The American Magazine*, April 1921. https://teslauniverse.com/nikola-tesla/articles/making-your-imagination-work-you.

Yates, Frances A. *The Art of Memory*. London: Bodley Head, 2014.

Young, Jon. *What the Robin Knows: How Birds Reveal the Secrets of the Natural World*. Illustrated edition. New York: Mariner Books, 2013.

Zhou, Feng, Christian Montag, Rayna Sariyska, Bernd Lachmann, Martin Reuter, Bernd Weber, Peter Trautner, Keith M. Kendrick, Sebastian Markett, and Benjamin Becker. 'Orbitofrontal Gray Matter Deficits as Marker of Internet Gaming Disorder: Converging Evidence from a Cross-Sectional and Prospective Longitudinal Design'. *Addiction Biology* 24, no. 1 (2019): 100–109. https://doi.org/10.1111/adb.12570.

Notes

_____

Introduction

1. A huge number of other children share the experience of feeling ignored by their parents in favour of smartphones. See Dona Matthews, 'Why Parents Really Need to Put Down Their Phones', Psychology Today, accessed 14 November 2020, https://www.psychologytoday.com/blog/going-beyond-intelligence/201711/why-parents-really-need-put-down-their-phones.

2. V. Rideout and M. B. Robb, 'The Common Sense Census: Media Use by Kids Age Zero to Eight, 2020' (San Francisco, CA: Common Sense Media, 2020), https://www.commonsensemedia.org/sites/default/files/uploads/research/2020_zero_to_eight_census_final_web.pdf.

3. Rideout and Robb.

4. As awareness of this troubling incentive structure spreads, the structure may be tweaked. Companies like Facebook are already making efforts to clean up their image and become less overtly harmful without losing profits. We should be wary of slightly different structures that may be problematic in their own ways. See Ben Tarnoff and Moira Weigel, 'Why Silicon Valley Can't Fix Itself', *The Guardian*, 3 May 2018, sec. News, https://www.theguardian.com/news/2018/may/03/why-silicon-valley-cant-fix-itself-tech-humanism.

Part I

1. The limitations and conclusion sections of this study highlight the complexity I am talking about (though it's pretty obvious when you think about internet use that it would not have uniform effects on the brain): Martin P. Paulus et al., 'Screen Media Activity and Brain Structure in Youth: Evidence for Diverse Structural Correlation Networks from the ABCD Study', *NeuroImage* 185 (15 January 2019): 10, https://doi.org/10.1016/j.neuroimage.2018.10.040.

2. This study was described and referenced in Kyle Langvardt, 'Regulating Habit-Forming Technology', *SSRN Electronic Journal*, 2019, 2, https://doi.org/10.2139/ssrn.3351936.

3. Michael B. Miller, *The Bon Marché: Bourgeois Culture and the Department Store, 1869-1920*

(Princeton, New Jersey: Princeton University Press, 1981), 50–51.

4. Meredith L. Clausen, 'The Department Store: Development of the Type', *Journal of Architectural Education* 39, no. 1 (1985): 20–29.

5. Victor Lebow, 'Price Competition in 1955', *Journal of Retailing*, Spring 1955.

6. Kathleen Davis, 'A (Kind of) Brief History of Marketing (Infographic)', Entrepreneur, 17 July 2013, https://www.entrepreneur.com/article/227438.

7. Robert D. Putnam, *Bowling Alone: Revised and Updated: The Collapse and Revival of American Community* (Simon and Schuster, 2020), 231.

8. Putnam, 217.

9. Putnam, 224.

10. Clay Shirky, 'Gin, Television, and Social Surplus', *Here Comes Everybody* (blog), 2 January 2011, https://web.archive.org/web/20110102193349/http://www.shirky.com/herecomeseve rybody/2008/04/looking-for-the-mouse.html.

11. James Burke, *Connections*, 1st American ed (Boston: Little, Brown and Company, 1978), 111–13.

12. My understanding of the history of the internet and computers mostly comes from conversations with a programmer who experienced the developments over the decades.

13. Alex Hern, 'Netflix's Biggest Competitor? Sleep', *The Guardian*, 18 April 2017, sec. Technology, https://www.theguardian.com/technology/2017/apr/18/netflix-competitor-sleep-uber-facebook.

14. Nir Eyal, *Indistractable: How to Control Your Attention and Choose Your Life* (Dallas, TX: BenBella Books, 2019).

15. This paper details two studies which found that absent-minded smartphone use was related to attention lapses in daily life: Jeremy Marty-Dugas et al., 'The Relation between Smartphone Use and Everyday Inattention.', *Psychology of Consciousness: Theory, Research, and Practice* 5, no. 1 (March 2018): 46–62, https://doi.org/10.1037/cns0000131.

16. Haley Sweetland Edwards, 'Silicon Valley Knows How to Program Human Behavior— for Better or Worse', *Time*, 23 April 2018, 36.

17. B. J. Fogg, *Persuasive Technology: Using Computers to Change What We Think and Do*, 1 edition

(Amsterdam; Boston: Morgan Kaufmann, 2002).

18. B. J. Fogg, 'About BJ Fogg, PhD Behaviour Scientist at Stanford University', BJ Fogg, PhD, accessed 12 October 2020, https://www.bjfogg.com/about.

19. B. J. Fogg, 'Persuasive Computers: Perspectives and Research Directions', in Proceedings of the SIGCHI Conference on Human Factors in Computing Systems - CHI '98 (the SIGCHI conference, Los Angeles, California, United States: ACM Press, 1998), 225–32, https://doi.org/10.1145/274644.274677.

20. Since that time, the name has changed; it is now called the Behaviour Design Lab.

21. Nellie Bowles, 'Addicted to Screens? That's Really a You Problem (Published 2019)', *The New York Times*, 6 October 2019, sec. Technology, https://www.nytimes.com/2019/10/06/technology/phone-screen-addiction-tech-nir-eyal.html.

22. Eyal's descriptions of the four stages of the Hook—Trigger, Action, Variable Reward, and Investment—can be found in Nir Eyal, *Hooked: How to Build Habit-Forming Products*, ed. Ryan Hoover, Rev. ed (New York, New York: Portfolio, 2014), 39–162.

23. C. B. Ferster and B. F. Skinner, *Schedules of Reinforcement* (Cambridge, Massachusetts: B.F. Skinner Foundation, 2014).

24. *Ramsay Brown, Boundless Mind at The Montgomery Summit 2018* (MontyTV, 2018), https://www.youtube.com/watch?v=TzDDpT11O_A.

25. Daniel Engber, 'Everything Is Crumbling', *Slate*, 6 March 2016, http://www.slate.com/articles/health_and_science/cover_story/2016/03/ego_depletion_an_influential_theory_in_psychology_may_have_just_been_debunked.html.

26. Feng Zhou et al., 'Orbitofrontal Gray Matter Deficits as Marker of Internet Gaming Disorder: Converging Evidence from a Cross-Sectional and Prospective Longitudinal Design', *Addiction Biology* 24, no. 1 (2019): 100–109, https://doi.org/10.1111/adb.12570.

27. Daria Joanna Kuss and Mark D. Griffiths, 'Internet Gaming Addiction: A Systematic Review of Empirical Research', *International Journal of Mental Health and Addiction* 10, no. 2 (1 April 2012): 278–96, https://doi.org/10.1007/s11469-011-9318-5; Xiao Lin et al., 'Abnormal Gray Matter and White Matter Volume in "Internet Gaming Addicts"', *Addictive Behaviors* 40 (1 January 2015): 137–43, https://doi.org/10.1016/j.addbeh.2014.09.010; Juliane Horvath et al., 'Structural and Functional Correlates of Smartphone Addiction', *Addictive Behaviors* 105 (1 June 2020): 106334, https://doi.org/10.1016/j.addbeh.2020.106334; Simone Kühn and Jürgen

Gallinat, 'Brains Online: Structural and Functional Correlates of Habitual Internet Use: Correlates of Internet Use', *Addiction Biology* 20, no. 2 (March 2015): 415–22, https://doi.org/10.1111/adb.12128; Qinghua He, Ofir Turel, and Antoine Bechara, 'Brain Anatomy Alterations Associated with Social Networking Site (SNS) Addiction', *Scientific Reports* 7, no. 1 (23 March 2017): 45064, https://doi.org/10.1038/srep45064; Kristiana Siste Kurniasanti et al., 'Internet Addiction: A New Addiction?', *Medical Journal of Indonesia* 28, no. 1 (8 May 2019): 82–91, https://doi.org/10.13181/mji.v28i1.2752.

28. There is a lot of evidence for links between intrinsic religiosity and self-control. See Ulrik Lyngs, 'What I Hate, That Do I: Religion as a Cultural Tool for Cognitive Control' (MA dissertation, Aarhus University, 2016).

29. B. J. Fogg, *Tiny Habits: The Small Changes That Change Everything*, Illustrated Edition (Boston: Houghton Mifflin Harcourt, 2019).

30. Ulrik Lyngs et al., 'Self-Control in Cyberspace: Applying Dual Systems Theory to a Review of Digital Self-Control Tools', in *Proceedings of the 2019 CHI Conference on Human Factors in Computing Systems - CHI '19* (the 2019 CHI Conference, Glasgow, UK: ACM Press, 2019), 1–18, https://doi.org/10.1145/3290605.3300361.

31. Jose Angelo Gallegos, 'The History and Evolution of Advertising', *The TINT Blog* (blog), 30 June 2016, https://www.tintup.com/blog/history-evolution-advertising-marketing/.

32. Lyngs et al., 'Self-Control in Cyberspace'.

33. This piece of advice is similar to one that appears in Nir Eyal's book *Indistractable* ('hack back external triggers'). I arrived at the concept before knowledge of that book, or Eyal's other book, *Hooked*, and have also encountered similar advice in several other places. The terms I use to explain it here, derived from the Hook model and also used in *Indistractable*, are chosen for consistency with previous chapters. *Indistractable* contains some more detailed ideas for how to 'hack back,' although these should not be hard to come up with yourself if you have practiced identifying sources of distraction.

34. Ang Liu and Tian Meng Li, 'Develop Habit-Forming Products Based on the Axiomatic Design Theory', *Procedia CIRP* 53 (2016): 119–24, https://doi.org/10.1016/j.procir.2016.07.035.

Part II

1. There was also, oddly, a clothing line called 'human packaging.' Which makes sense, I suppose, when we are the product being sold.

2. Sean Hollister, 'Mattel Is Making an Amazon Echo That Understands Your Kids, Too', CNET, accessed 28 October 2020, https://www.cnet.com/reviews/aristotle-by-nabi-preview/.

3. For the Waorani and their sense of smell, as well as the Wayfinders, see Wade Davis, 'Dreams from Endangered Cultures' (TED), accessed 28 November 2020, https://www.ted.com/talks/wade_davis_dreams_from_endangered_cultures; For more on the Polynesian Wayfinders, see Wade Davis, *The Wayfinders: Why Ancient Wisdom Matters in the Modern World*, First Edition (Toronto: House of Anansi Press, 2009); I am not certain where in Davis's work I came across the piece about the Inuit cloud-reflection map. It may have been Wade Davis, *Light at the Edge of the World: A Journey Through the Realm of Vanishing Cultures*, Fourth Impression edition (Vancouver: Douglas & McIntyre, 2007).

4. Jon Young, *What the Robin Knows: How Birds Reveal the Secrets of the Natural World*, Illustrated edition (New York: Mariner Books, 2013).

5. Michael Schulson, 'If the Internet Is Addictive, Why Don't We Regulate It?', Aeon, accessed 2 October 2020, https://aeon.co/essays/if-the-internet-is-addictive-why-don-t-we-regulate-it.

6. David Abram, *The Spell of the Sensuous: Perception and Language in a More-Than-Human World* (New York: Pantheon Books, 1996), 58.

7. M. K. Wisehart, 'Making Your Imagination Work for You', The American Magazine, April 1921, https://teslauniverse.com/nikola-tesla/articles/making-your-imagination-work-you.

8. Frances A. Yates, *The Art of Memory* (London: Bodley Head, 2014).

9. Lynne Kelly, *Knowledge and Power in Prehistoric Societies: Orality, Memory and the Transmission of Culture* (New York: Cambridge University Press, 2015).

10. Lynne Kelly, *Memory Craft: Improve Your Memory Using the Most Powerful Methods from around the World*, 2019.

11. Kelly, 2019.

12. Kelly, *Knowledge and Power in Prehistoric Societies*.

13. Kep Kee Loh and Ryota Kanai, 'How Has the Internet Reshaped Human Cognition?', *The Neuroscientist* 22, no. 5 (October 2016): 506–20, https://doi.org/10.1177/1073858415595005.

14. I have tweaked these from the Medieval art of memory. The language is modernised,

and I made it slightly more general to show how it can apply beyond memory to habit, attention, etc. See: Yates, *The Art of Memory*, 85.

15. 'Google Can Bring You Back 100,000 Answers. A Librarian Can Bring You Back the Right One', *Quote Investigator* (blog), accessed 24 November 2020, https://quoteinvestigator.com/2016/04/23/library/.

16. Plato, 'Phaedrus', The Internet Classics Archive, accessed 18 November 2019, http://classics.mit.edu/Plato/phaedrus.html.

17. Plato.

Part III

1. Ann Williamson and R. Friswell, 'Fatigue and Driving: Disentangling the Relative Effects of Time of Day and Sleep Deprivation' (2008 Australasian Road Safety Research, Policing and Education Conference, Adelaide, South Australia: University of New South Wales, 2008), 7.

2. Schulson, 'If the Internet Is Addictive, Why Don't We Regulate It?'

3. Eyal, *Indistractable*.

4. Schulson, 'If the Internet Is Addictive, Why Don't We Regulate It?'

5. Rideout and Robb, 'The Common Sense Census: Media Use by Kids Age Zero to Eight, 2020'.

6. V. Rideout and M. B. Robb, 'The Common Sense Census: Media Use by Tweens and Teens, 2019' (San Francisco, CA: Common Sense Media, 2019), https://www.commonsensemedia.org/sites/default/files/uploads/research/2019-census-8-to-18-full-report-updated.pdf.

7. 'Instagram Swaps out Its "Activity" Tab for "Shop" in New Global Test', *TechCrunch* (blog), accessed 28 November 2020, https://social.techcrunch.com/2020/07/07/instagram-swaps-out-its-activity-tab-for-shop-in-new-global-test/.